Preface

SUCCESS

SUCCESS STAIRWAY

A spiritual journey of self-discovery

Success is first a BEING choice and then a doing thing, yet most of us have it backwards. The success formula is, and always has been, BE DO HAVE, not DO HAVE BE. And if you want success far beyond the ordinary, you'll want to learn why the process of becoming wealthy is actually a spiritual journey of self-discovery.

Contrary to popular opinion, God wants you to be wealthy. And since that idea is probably far outside your comfort zone (your Belief System) you'll either have to put this book back on the shelf or read it with the intention of perhaps changing your mind about some ideas that have kept you poorer than you've wanted to be.

From rags to riches

30 years ago, four-year old Thach Nguyen and his family arrived in the United States from Vietnam, with only the clothes on their backs, a small cardboard suitcase and $100. Because Thach's father worked for the United States during the Vietnamese war, they were forced to leave their country when the North Vietnamese took over.

On his first day in school, the other kids made fun of the way Thach was dressed. He made up his mind, then, to prove he was as good as those other kids.

Years later, still proving himself good enough, Thach was the number-one producer for John Scott L. Real Estate, and had been for five years in a row. His income when I first talked to Thach on the phone was $350,000 a month.

Why success is a spiritual journey
Then, Thach learned why his success up until then had actually been a spiritual journey. In the BEING Workshop, we showed Thach how to double his income with half the effort, using the spiritual power he already had.

In his first eight-week BEING Workshop, Thach took his income from $350,000 to $750,000 a month. His income has doubled and redoubled. Now, Thach's main mission in life is not about making money, it's about making a difference and he is accomplishing his goal. But the money keeps flowing!

The message in this book is intended to change your reality concept in a way that could make you many times richer, happier and more successful than you've ever dreamed possible.

Fifteen millionaires helped create this book
The ideas for this book were first tested and proven in a workshop created especially for a group of fifteen participants who were already successful far beyond the average person's dreams. Each of the fifteen was a millionaire, intending to increase his or her income to a million dollars a month.

To God or As God

This elite group first came to us as referrals from Thach. His testimony, along with our offer to show them how to double their incomes while working half the time, persuaded 15 participants to sign up for that workshop.

In making good on that offer, I had to custom design the workshop assignments to their needs. Although I had been teaching prosperity workshops since 1952, it became necessary to grow my own consciousness in order to teach this special group some new tricks.

Most of them doubled their incomes or more, as promised, and in addition, found ample free time to enjoy their life, their families, and their money. This book is a compilation of that workshop material and assignments.

With a power they already had

You see, we didn't give those millionaires a power they didn't already have. We merely showed fifteen already successful people how to use their personal power to attract success as opposed to crunching it out to make it happen. Net result: far greater success, but without the usual stress.

All fifteen had a powerful spiritual awakening in the process.

Whether you are seeking more self-confidence, further success or a spiritual awakening, the lessons to be learned from reading this book will pleasantly surprise you. What will surprise you most is that success in any form, financial or otherwise, must be preceded by a spiritual awakening.

Success is first a BEING choice and then a doing thing. So come along with me. Let's walk the spiritual path to success together. And I believe you will walk the path to glory.

Warning Disclaimer

This book is designed to provide information in regard to the subject matter covered. It is sold with the understanding that the publisher and the author are not engaged in rendering legal, accounting, or other professional services. If legal or other expert assistance is required, the services of a competent professional should be sought.

The purpose of this book is to educate and entertain. The Author and DAR Publishing shall have neither liability nor responsibility to any person or entity with respect to loss or damage caused or alleged to be caused, directly or indirectly by the information contained in this book.

If you do not wish to be bound by the above, you may return this book to the publisher for full refund.

TO God or AS God
By Darel Rutherford

DAR PUBLISHING

Published by: 7116 Arroyo Del Oso NE
Albuquerque, N.M. 87109

Copyright October, 2006 by Darel Rutherford
Printed in the United States of America
ISBN - 13 : 978 - 0 - 9670540 - 4 - 9
ISBN - 10 : 0 - 9670540 - 4 – 4

About The Author

Darel Rutherford, self-made millionaire, public speaker, BEING coach, and BEING Workshop presenter, is the author of ten books; the most famous of which are BEING THE SOLUTION and SO WHY AREN'T YOU RICH.

Darel's SUCCESS WITHOUT STRESS, MASTERING YOUR LIFE, and MILLION-DOLLAR-A-MONTH BEING Workshops have helped thousands realize their goals while eliminating the usual stress and effort most would assume normal for the super-successful

The ideas in this book were inspired by millionaires, taking Darel's six-month, Mastering Your Life Workshop; all wanting an abundant and fulfilling life that included inspiring and helping others realize their dreams as well.

You'll be reading the ways in which they manifested amazing results while learning how to attract success easily, with joy and satisfaction, instead of the usual make-it-happen, crunch-it-out approach to creating wealth and success. Additionally, all reported better health and happier relationships, something few believe possible to achieve while manifesting wealth.

Darel's not shy about his mission to transform the world by teaching and inspiring others to become powerful, productive transformers of those wanting a better life. With his books, coaching program and workshops he shows them the easy way to manifest prosperity for themselves and others.

Acknowledgments

First I'd like to acknowledge my daughter, Sherry who read, critiqued, and edited this book from its beginning. As my office manager, Sherry gave me the time to write this book by magically and efficiently handling all the details of the business of marketing and managing BEING Workshops and book sales.

Next I want to express my appreciation for Deborah Ivanoff, my friend, co-host and head coach for the BEING Workshops since the beginning. I couldn't begin to count the ways Deborah has contributed to the creation of this book.

I especially want to thank my friend, Thach Nguyen, for recommending the BEING Workshop to so many of his already successful friends. We promised to show his friends how to double their incomes with half the effort.

In order to keep that promise, it became necessary to grow our own consciousness and customize the workshop to their needs.

Then last, but not least, my thanks to the participants of our first six-month Mastering Your Life Workshop. Their active participation, their desires for growth, and their response to the Workshop homework created the content of this book. Some of those ideas were new to me, but they've all been put to the test and proven to work without fail.

To God or As God

And in the process, several millionaires learned how to double their incomes with half the effort. And they all now celebrate the fact that they finally have the time to enjoy their lives, their family and their money.

Listed below are the names of those participants who allowed me to share their names.

- Chris Larmer
- Eric Elegado
- Esther Navarro
- Greg Harrelson
- Gus Islas
- Jackie Pasciak
- James Tjoa
- Jeff Quintin
- Joe DiRaffaele
- Judy Banfield
- Mary Hampton
- Scott Friedman
- Scott Umstead
- Shannan Fogle
- Tamara Dean
- Tammie Johnson
- Thach Nguyen
- Venny Saucedo

CLIP ART COURTESY OF:
MICROSOFT OFFICE and REAL DRAW

Although the following testimonies are praise for another book and for the BEING Workshop, you may want to read it as real testimony for how powerful and life-changing the ideas in this book could be for you.

Workshop Participant testimony

I was able to manifest any end result I wanted. I went from earning $750,000 per year to over $1,000,000 per month. Thanks, Darel.

--Thach Nguyen

I am DOING less work and making more money than ever before.

--Chris Larmer

Thank you so much for all that you have done for me and my ego. The BEING CHOICE!!!!

--Eric Elegado

I've been part of the BEING Workshops for 8 years. ...life just keeps getting better and better for me. I have become someone I once only dreamed about.

--Deborah Ivanoff

I never imagined that I could 'Advance to Go' and collect my $200 so easy. I can't wait for his next lesson.

--Greg Harrelson

... my net income has tripled, and my net worth has more than doubled. All of this has happened with far less stress in my life.

--Jackie Pasciak

To God or As God

I have experienced such growth in my business and investments that I have decided to retire in three years. (I am 37 now).
                                                                    --James Tjoa

...we have earned more in 45 days then we did all of last year. What's truly great is that the income we earned last year is in the top 1% nationally.
                                                                    --Joe DiRaffaele
                                                                    --Shannan Fogle

I have acquired a new sense of myself, embraced abundance consciousness, and feel in tune with life.
                                                                    --Judy Banfield

A newer relationship evolved into a wonderful, loving, committed marriage because of the growth I experience while in the BEING WORKSHOP.
                                                                    --Scott Friedman

I am now experiencing true fulfillment in every phase of my life and magnetically attracting things I thought mostly belonged to others.
                                                                    --Scott B. Umstead

Worry used to consume me. Not anymore. I live my life in a free mode. I know I can do what I want to.
                                                                    --Tamara Dean

I am forever grateful to you for showing me all the joy and light that was within me all along!!
                                                                    --Tammie Johnson

You truly made a difference in my life. I thank GOD daily for putting you into my life. I wish everyone could learn these life changing principles.
                                                                    --Venny Saucedo

For their full testimony, turn to the last chapter in this book.

Table of Contents

Part III:
Tools to Stay Out of Ego's Traps ..126

Part IV: Life With Spirit In Charge 171

Your Life, a Fairytale

One day a caterpillar woke up, discovered it had wings and flew

Your life is a fairytale in which you can truly have anything you want from life if you have the self-confidence to choose it and the self-worth to accept it.

You want to BE healthier, happier and more prosperous? Just choose to BE. The only reason you don't already have that benefit in your life is; you don't believe life could be that simple. Well it is!

You'll learn from reading this book that, healthy, happy, and prosperous are simply BEING choices. Your circumstances, (good or bad) are merely a reflection of what you believe and who you've chosen to BE.

You want to BE healthier, happier and wealthy? Just change your mind about what you believe and make that new BEING choice.

Life really is that simple, so hold on to your hat and we'll show you the way to a better life!

Find your wings and fly!

Part I

The Power To BE

...and How It Works

You and I were created in the image and likeness of God. If you don't believe me, check your bible. That's good news, but it is also God's cosmic joke on you, because at the time of putting a part of Himself in us, He also gave us amnesia.

The power of God in you is the BEING Principle—the power to choose who you will be. This is an awesome power, but it is not serving you with awesome manifestations, because you've forgotten who you are and that you have that power.

You also have another great power, the power to attract. You seem to have forgotten that one too, but even so, it's working right now, attracting who and what belongs with you.

The way that power in you works is: once you've chosen, the Universe, the Law, or whatever you choose to call it, will automatically deliver who and whatever belongs in the reality of that BEING choice.

In other words, you have the power to create any new reality you can dream up and have it manifest, as if by magic. You have the power to make the quantum leap out of poverty and into riches, just by choosing it, and the Universe must deliver on that BEING choice.

Unfortunately, you have amnesia. You've forgotten you have that power.

What you'll learn in Part I of this book will help you understand what that power looks like in you and how it works. You'll learn there's no limit to your manifesting powers, other than those foolish ones you've set for yourself.

Your reading of the following nine chapters will awaken that sleeping giant within you and start you on your way to manifesting your dream reality.

Chapters
1. The Quantum Leap
2. TO God or AS God
3. How Prayers Get Answered
4. The Will of God—God's Plan For You
5. A Winner's Attitude
6. What's Stopping You?
7. Trapped In Your Act
8. Knowing Your Why
9. The Baby Step

Once you've learned how to be a god in your own life, once you're ready to make your new BEING commitment, you'll want to put your enthusiasm on hold until you've read Parts II and III on ego's traps and how to deal with them.

In Part II you'll learn why your ego is ready to sabotage your desired change. You'll learn why any previous attempts to succeed may have failed, and in Part III you'll learn how to deal with your built in resistance to change.

The Quantum Leap

A Leap of Faith

A giant leap of faith

A man's business is on the brink of failure. One more month like the last two, and he will be closing the doors of that business for good. As he locks up to go home, that Saturday at noon, he is quite certain his employees must already be looking for other jobs. He feels sad and totally disheartened by the thought of losing his business.

Then on Sunday, while reading an inspirational self-help book, a truth dawns on him that totally changes his perspective on life. Almost instantaneously, the man is filled with enthusiasm, joy and excitement. What life-changing truth completely transformed his perspective?

He learned a truth about life, a principle that allowed him to choose out of failure into a winning attitude. He chose success and in the blink of an eye, went from a sad-sack to a can't-fail perspective. His winning attitude turned his failing business into a roaring success almost overnight.

So, what really happened here? Was this a so-called miracle? No. It was merely applied principle. He discovered a truth that allowed him to take a quantum leap up in consciousness. He suddenly realized that he could change his mind about who he would be, and that BEING shift would automatically solve his problem!

The Quantum Leap

Quantum leap is a term used in quantum physics to describe the explosive and unpredictable movements of a photon, the smallest known particle of matter. The photon's rapid moves seem almost magical as it quantum leaps from one place to another so fast it seems to be in both places at once.

Metaphorically speaking, the photon seems to get from home base to third plate without touching the bases in between. Its moves are so fast you can't see them happening. Science calls these photon moves, the quantum leap. I wonder, is the photon a tiny consciousness choosing to BE somewhere else, and then arriving there instantaneously? Hmm?

That's an interesting idea, because we human beings also occasionally take quantum leaps. In the blink of an eye, we can take ourselves out of one reality concept and into another by simply changing our minds about who we will be. And that self-concept change is actually a quantum leap in consciousness!

You've done it before

You've taken many such quantum leaps in your life time, but somehow you keep forgetting that you have that power—that capability. Your quantum leaps were those times when, in the spur of the moment, you decided to change your mind about who you would be. Your commitment to a new way of being you was a quantum leap out of one reality into another.

Think about having the power to choose for a moment and you'll remember some of the times when you made those leaps of faith.

One of those times was when, as a crawling baby, you decided to get up off your knees and walk. Did you know how before you decided to walk? Did not knowing how stop you? No. In spite of not knowing the how-to, you decided to get up and walk.

I want you to see that in choosing to go from a crawler to a walker, you made the quantum leap in consciousness. And like flipping a switch, with a simple BEING choice, you transformed out of the reality of a crawler into that of a walker.

Of course, it took a little while for you to get the hang of it, but I want you to see that once you'd made up your mind to walk, the outcome was inevitable. Allow yourself to see that the results of a new BEING commitment are as certain to manifest, as night follows day, and then choose. Why not apply the BEING solution to your current situation?

You need to know that you are capable in any moment of now, to take a quantum leap of faith that will move you out of boredom and into a life of joy, satisfaction and enthusiasm. And, once you've committed to that new way of being you, the outcome is always undeniable. You've done it many times before now, and you can do it again and again.

Another example of when you've boldly taken yourself out of one reality and into another was that time when you made

The Quantum Leap

up your mind to ride a bicycle. At the time, this may have seemed to be a "doing" choice—something you would do. But that's not what really happened here. What really happened is, you chose to BE a bicycle rider, and that BEING decision was a quantum leap of faith!

And you didn't know how

Think about it! Before that first ride, did you know how to ride a bicycle? No. And you probably wondered, before you tried, how anyone can learn to ride a bike if no one can tell you how. But, did not knowing how stop you? No! You just got on the bicycle and started pedaling like crazy, hoping you wouldn't fall.

Did you fall a few times? Probably yes. Did falling stop you from getting up and trying again? No, of course not! You might want to let yourself see that riding a bike for the first time was a quantum leap of faith.

You might want to use that example out of your past to remind yourself that you can do it again. You are truly capable of taking the quantum leap out of your worst problem into a reality in which that problem is solved. You'll do that without knowing how the problem will be solved.

I'm assuming you have a problem that needs a solution. The solution, of course, is that quantum leap into the reality of a new way of BEING you, in which the problem is already solved.

If you're not happy with current circumstances, you might want to assume the winner's attitude you had when you decided to get off your knees and walk, or when you decided to climb on and ride that bike. You didn't know how then, either, but you chose anyway.

The point is that you don't need to know the "How-To," before taking your quantum leap into that dream reality.

I made a BEING choice
In 1952, as part of a study group discussing the book, *Think and Grow Rich*, I announced my intention to become a millionaire. But then I got busy running my business and promptly forgot I had set that goal. Two years later, a participant in that study group asked me,

> *How are you doing on your goal to become a millionaire?*

I answered,

> *I don't know, but I'll check it out and let you know the next time I see you.*

When I did the numbers, I found I was half-way toward my second million. The point of this story is that I made the quantum leap out of a non-millionaire's reality into the millionaire's reality without knowing how it would happen.

All I did was say, "Yes"
After reviewing my progress and looking back at that quantum leap of faith, I was embarrassed to realize that I had done absolutely nothing to initiate any of the steps I had taken in becoming a millionaire.

The process involved several investments over that two-year period. But for each investment made, someone else had come up with the idea. I merely said, "Yes, yes, and yes" to those opportunities as they showed up.

Two lessons can be learned from this example:
1. You don't need to know the "How-to" before you take the quantum leap of faith.

2. Once you've chosen, the Universe will deliver whatever belongs in the reality of that BEING choice. All you have to do is say yes to those opportunities as they show up.

And you can do it again

You've been taking quantum leaps out of one reality concept into another all your life without knowing the "How-To." So, let this chapter be your reminder. You DO have that capability—you've always had it.

Isn't it time you solved your worst problem with your next quantum leap? You DO know how to leap, you know. It's simple, you just choose out of that problem reality and into the reality of being a _____, (you fill in the blank) and then get on that bike and pedal like crazy.

You could choose, right now to BE a millionaire. It's as simple as changing your mind. You can change your mind, can't you?

Every out-of-the-box BEING decision you've ever made in life was a quantum leap in consciousness. That means you changed your mind about who you would be, and then practiced the DOING until you perfected your new role.

With each new BEING choice, you've leaped out of "I can't" into "I can" in the snap of your fingers.

What inspired you to leap?

Now, let's talk about what it was that inspired you to take your quantum leaps in the past. In most of those cases, your inspiration would have been the idea that you really could have something you dearly wanted—something you assumed would make you happy.

To God or As God

You made those leaps of faith because you expected to be happier once the quality of your life got better in some way. So, did having what you wanted make you happy? I doubt it, because having stuff isn't what real happiness is made of.

The bluebird of happiness can't be caught nor caged. Chase it, and it flies away. But choose to BE happy, with no conditions attached, and that bluebird will land on your shoulder. With that in mind, you might want to stop chasing happiness and just choose to BE happy, no matter what.

They're not the same

The usual problem with happiness-seekers is in believing that happiness and satisfaction are one and the same. They're not.

Satisfaction is merely the completion of anything attempted, while happiness is simply a way of being—a BEING choice. You can't have satisfaction until you've actually ridden the bike, so to speak, but you can choose to be happy in any moment of now, no matter what the circumstances.

I want you to see that riding that bike for the first time gave you a great deal of satisfaction, but being satisfied didn't make you happy. Not that you couldn't be happy riding a bike for the first time, but in confusing happiness and satisfaction as one and the same, you'll be disappointed, time after time, because satisfaction never lasts.

A kid's dream come true

I'll never forget how happy I felt my first day in my new job as soda jerk-delivery boy for Butts Drug Store, in downtown Albuquerque, N.M. My boss said, "Darel, eat all the ice cream you want." Wow, this was a kid's dream come true! I was 15 years old the day I overindulged, which spoiled my appetite for ice cream for a long time to come.

You see, I truly thought having all the ice cream I could eat would make me happy. But what do you suppose happened to my happiness when I became too full of ice cream? And when I had satisfied my hunger for ice cream, did I stop eating? NO! And did eating more ice cream make me more satisfied? No. Of course not.

The point is, if your motivation for those quantum leaps was to find happiness, you've been barking up the wrong tree. The bluebird of happiness isn't up in that tree or anyplace else you'd care to look for it. But it'll come sit on you shoulder once you've stopped chasing it.

If your motivation for taking the quantum leaps is to seek satisfaction and growth in consciousness, you're on the right track. And since satisfaction is experienced only on the completion of anything attempted, you'll be finding more and more ways to satisfy your hunger for growth.

The Game of Life is designed so that you'll be inspired to take one quantum leap after the other. And your journey through life will be a great deal more enjoyable if you'll allow yourself to see that you're seeking satisfaction, not happiness. A change of circumstances can't make you happy; happiness is just a BEING choice.

The quantum leap
Choosing out of unhappiness into happiness is a quantum leap you could take at any moment of now. Why not choose happiness now? The quantum leap happens any time you change your mind about who you are, or who you will be. It also happens once you've changed your mind about what

you believe. That quantum leap, in each case, will be a transformation in consciousness.

If what you learn while reading this chapter changes your mind about who you are and what you believe, that reality concept change would be a quantum leap in consciousness. And once you've taken your leap of faith, that reality concept change is guaranteed to transform the quality of your life forever! Are you ready for that?

Quantum physics

In researching for this chapter, I purchased and read several books on quantum physics. As the non-scientist, I found them rather boring, for the most part. But while wading through the boredom, I learned why certain physics experiments have scientists rethinking their theories about how the human consciousness functions.

This new physics has incredible implications concerning you, your potential and the creative power of your mind. I'm sure after reading this you'll want to change your frame of reference about the Universe and how you fit into it. So, let's see if I, as a non-scientist, can explain quantum physics in a way that changes your reality concept, and inspires you to take your own quantum leap of faith.

"Quantum" is a Latin word meaning, "how much." Quantum physics is the branch of physics that deals with subatomic systems. The smallest known measurable subatomic entity is a particle of light, called a photon. What's amazing about a photon is that it can show up as either a wave or a particle. Why is that exciting?

It seems the photon is capable of being a wave or a particle, depending on what the observer expects to see. If the experimenter is intending to measure the photon as a wave, it shows up as a wave; but if an observer expects to see particles, the photon will appear as a particle.

In other words, in quantum theory research, the intent of the observer actually influences the outcome experiment. This is exciting news which, in my opinion, gives us reliable scientific evidence, proving our thoughts DO in fact, have the power to affect matter.

The philosophers had it right
What philosophers have been saying for ages is now proven by the new science …that our thoughts have the power to affect the physical world…that our expectations are truly a creative force in the universe!

Until quantum physics, science had never really accepted the philosopher's point of view, that consciousness has a real effect on our material reality. And even though many scientists wholeheartedly embrace the consciousness theory of quantum measurement, some are still skeptical. And here's why.

If we hypothesize that quantum physics laws govern the physical universe, then we must accept that human consciousness, through the power of intention, influences the outcome of these quantum theory experiments. It would seem, then, that we now have scientific evidence proving that we humans do, in fact, have the power to influence the quality of our circumstances.

But some scientists would say this view of the quantum theory leads us to the conclusion that nothing is real outside our consciousness. An example of this point of view is Bertrand Russell's comments back in 1956:

It has begun to seem that matter, like the Cheshire Cat, is becoming gradually diaphanous [transparent] *and nothing is left but the grin, caused, presumably, by amusement at those who still think it's there.*

Isn't it interesting that, up until quantum physics, scientific experiments had never made the human soul (the spirit of god in man) a part of the equation? Now it seems that physics, the most objective of all sciences, has put the soul of man at the very center of our newest understanding of the universe.

As you read on, you'll find ample reason to believe with certainty that you are far more powerful than you have allowed yourself to imagine. And, if that's so, what will you do with that power?

Notice if you feel a tinge of fear as you think about being more powerful. That's because your greatest fear in life is that you will discover how powerful you really are!

Important enough to repeat
Choosing out of unhappiness into happiness is a quantum leap, a BEING choice you could take at any moment of now. Why not choose happiness now?

The quantum leap will happen any time you can change your mind about who you are, or about what you believe. Your quantum leap—by just changing your mind—will be a transformation in consciousness.

Be ye reborn by the renewing of your mind
--the apostle Paul

The Quantum Leap

If what you learned while reading this chapter has changed your mind about who you are and what you believe, that reality concept change is a quantum leap in consciousness. And once you've taken that leap of faith, your new reality concept change is guaranteed to transform the quality of your life forever! Are you ready for that?

In summary

The power to BE

In the blink of an eye, we humans can take ourselves out of one reality concept and into another by simply changing our minds about who we will be. And that self-concept change is actually a quantum leap in consciousness!

You've taken many such quantum leaps in your life time, but somehow you keep forgetting that you have that power—that capability.

Your quantum leaps were those times when, in the spur of the moment, you decided to change your mind about who you would be. Like when you learned to walk, ride a bike or ski, your commitment to a new way of being was a powerful quantum leap out of one reality and into another.

Think about having the power to choose for a moment and remember some of the other times when you made those leaps of faith. And having remembered, you can do it again.

Are you ready to take that leap of faith into better health, prosperous living and loving relationships? In the next chapter, you'll learn where you got the power to take the quantum leap into that better reality.

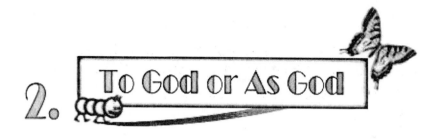

2. To God or As God

God's Cosmic Joke on You

God's joke on humanity:

Make man a god,
then have him forget he's a god

That's right! God put a part of Himself in each of us, then gave us amnesia. So, from time to time, as we play at the Game of Life, we'll have a spiritual awakening, find our power, use it to manifest some miracle, and then forget, yet once again who we really are.

The problem with that is: When you are an amnesia victim, you haven't lost your power; you've just forgotten you have it. As a god, every word you speak and every thought you think is a powerful prayer that must be answered by a universe that doesn't know how to say "No".

Can you imagine how powerful you'd be and what kind of miracles you could manifest if you could just wake up and stay conscious! Wow!

Warning!
What you are about to read could transform your life forever, but you probably won't get it. I'm about to tell you that you are powerful beyond your wildest dreams, but you probably won't believe me, because you are already programmed to believe otherwise.

You see, you have a reality filter in place—we all do. That filter is designed to screen out any and all information that does not fit what you already believe. What you currently believe to be true is your *reality concept.*

What you may not know is that your reality concept determines who and what belongs in the reality of your current point of view about life. What you have in your life is there, because it belongs with you, and what you want that's missing is not there for the opposite reason—it doesn't belong with you.

So, are you ready for this?
I'm assuming you'd like a change of circumstances. Sorry. The change you want can't happen until you've changed your reality concept. You are locked into a reality and a set of circumstances that cannot change until you change your mind about what you believe to be true.

Or to put it another way: in order for the message in this book to make any real difference in your life, it would have to be contrary to what you already believed, wouldn't it? Let's face it: I've already rattled your **B**elief **S**ystem cage.

So, think about that for a moment and ask yourself:

- o Can you be open to an idea, a reality concept that's totally outside the box and contrary to what you've always thought to be true?
- o Can you be open to the possibility that some of the things you now believe may not be true?
- o Can you really read this book with an open mind?

If not, and if you're not ready to learn a cage-rattling truth that may take you outside your current reality concept, then you might be better off to set this book aside and walk away.

The truth that will set you free

This is a truth that will truly change your life and set you free if you're ready for it.

What you'll learn here will either have you succeeding in all ways beyond your wildest imagination, or it will upset you—and it may do both.

Some will find the message in this book controversial, even sacrilegious. In fact, they nailed Christ to the cross for attempting to bring us this same truth over 2000 years ago. They weren't ready for it back then: I'm assuming you are ready for it, or you wouldn't be reading this.

If I'm reading the signs right—the book titles in book stores— the world is ready for a paradigm shift—a spiritual awakening. I say it's time for a consciousness change—not just yours, but the whole world's!

So, if you are truly ready to learn the truth, you're about to have a spiritual awakening.

But you did hear it in Sunday school

If you attended Sunday school as a kid, you surely learned that you were *created in the image and likeness of God.*

- o But what does that bible quote mean—really?
- o Have you truly considered the profound nature of that truth?
- o Have you let the idea of being a *likeness of God* sink in and be anything more than empty words?

"Created in His image and likeness" means just that, that you were created to be like God with God-like powers. And you are powerful, whether you've realized it or not. God duplicated Himself in you and me and that gives us the power to create our own individualized realities.

We've been using that power, creating one reality after another all our lives, without a clue that we had the power and were misusing it. While you're assessing that awesome truth, let's look at one more bible quote that may help you understand and learn how to use your God-like powers.

A word of power

In your bible you'll find, *In the beginning was **the word** and the word was **of God**, and the word was **God**.* What does that quote actually mean? What powerful word did God say from which He created the whole universe—what word did he say that was also a name for God?

The word of power is, *I am.* God said, *I am,* and created the world, the stars, and the whole universe out of Himself. He then created mankind and gave us dominion. He gave us the power to say *I am...* and complete our BEING statements in any way we choose.

To God or As God

Your *I am* power is the power of God in you, expressing life in and through you—as you.

As part of the whole

That makes God a part of you and you a part of God. Think about it! He individualized Himself in you and me, and this makes you an individualization of God. If this idea isn't real for you yet, just know that He lives in your heart and awaits your discovery.

Of course, that doesn't make you God Almighty, any more than a drop of water is the ocean, but being part of that ocean—an individualization of God—means you have some pretty amazing creative powers you have not yet understood nor learned to use wisely.

Science of Mind

Ernest Holmes, in his <u>Science of Mind Text Book</u>, boiled this awesome truth down to a simple statement when he wrote, *God as man, in man is man.*

Allow yourself to ponder the idea that God is a part of you. See if you can accept the possibility that God experiences life in and through all His creations. Then bring that thought home and see if you can allow yourself to accept the idea that God, as Spirit, experiences life in and through you as you.

A pretty breathtaking thought, isn't it?

The BEING principle

So, what does this power of God in you look like? And if you have the power, why haven't you been aware of it until now?

Why haven't you used that awesome power to make yourself rich and powerful?

The power of God in you shows up as the BEING Principle; that's the power to choose who you will be. You do that (choose who to BE) every time you think. That's why we become what we think about—an awesome power, whether you've realized it or not.

Your problem has been that you were not aware you were choosing who to BE with every thought.

Every thought a prayer

And you were also not aware that every thought is a powerful prayer that must and will be answered by a Universe that does not know how to say "no." The prayer-answering process is on automatic. You'll learn more about that in the next chapter.

You see, every time you've chosen who to BE by choosing what to think, the Universe has delivered up on that BEING choice. Your prayers (BEING choices) are answered automatically by another spiritual law, the Law of Attraction. You've been using the power to BE all your life, totally unaware that, out of ignorance, you were at the effect of your thoughts, positive or negative.

As an individualization of God, your thoughts are powerful beyond belief! What would happen if you took charge of your thinking? Can you even imagine how great your life would be if you learned how to use that awesome power to create a life of joy, happiness and prosperity?

Once you've learned to intentionally apply the BEING Principle as a solution to all problems, you'll easily manifest the good life in more ways than you've dreamed possible. In acquiring the power to manifest at will, you'll be stepping out of your current self-limiting self-concept and into a new reality of self-confidence and personal power.

But not until you've proven it

If the idea that you are an individualization of God excites you, congratulations! You've just latched on to a truth that could forever change your life, but maybe not. Knowing this truth won't substantially change the quality of your life until you've internalized it and made it real through measurable manifested results.

A very large gap exists between our believing something intellectually and knowing it from experience. In other words, acceptance of this truth can be an intellectual trap—that of believing the quality of your life will change, automatically, simply because you've learned this truth.

Your new-found understanding will not automatically change your life, any more than you'd be a pilot if you read a book on aerodynamics and truly understood the principle that keeps the plane in the air.

You'll be a pilot only after you've put your butt in the pilot's seat and experienced the thrill of flying by the seat of your pants. And you won't truly know you are an individualization of God, until you've proved that to yourself by manifesting positive evidence in the form of measurable results.

The power of God in you works for you when it works through you--as you. Your god-power is set in motion each time you choose to BE YOU in a brand new way. In other words, the quality of your life will change for the better when you've learned to BE the answer to your own prayer.

And while BEING the solution to your own problems, you are actually being GOD in your own life. That may sound sacrilegious to some, but I'm not saying anything new here.

Christ tried to tell us the same thing over 2000 years ago. They nailed Him to the cross for saying, *I and my father are one, and ye are my brethren.* I read His meaning to be, *I am one with God and so are you.* And He also said, *The kingdom of God is within you.*

So, what I'm telling you is not contrary to what He was teaching us. I'm merely interpreting that truth in a way that will, if you can accept it as your truth, allow you to find your way beyond believing to experiential knowing.

What have you done with this truth?
Before we move on, let's look at the fact that you've probably heard all of this before. How many times have you heard or read that you were *made in His image and likeness?* Let's look at how you've processed that information each time it came to your attention before now.

You did exactly what almost everyone does with it. You discarded it into file 13, (the round file), or you filed it away somewhere in the folder labeled "non-experience." In essence, you rejected the idea of being god-like as irrelevant, unusable data.

Each time you've heard this truth before, the analytical thinker in you (not your Being) ran it past your reality concept filter, and simply discarded it or set it aside. This was, because being powerful didn't match your self-concept or your pre-conceived notions about life in general.

Think about it! Haven't you, in reading this, reacted to the idea of you being powerful? Didn't your ego mind-chatter come up with a pile of evidence to prove your powerlessness? That self-talk was your ego mind's reality filter at work. We all have an idea filter in place, and it's always working to keep us confined in our current reality concept (the cage of self-imposed limitations).

Turn off the filter

So, before you read on, you might want to see if you've turned off your reality-concept filter. What you've read so far, and what I'm about to tell you will profoundly change and improve the quality of your life, but only if you are ready to accept it as YOUR truth.

If you are truly determined to come out of that box and are ready to manifest that change in your life, this book will change your life. And you can take that promise to the bank!

But, even now, as you read this information your ego mind stands ready to press the reject button if what you're reading is not a perfect match for what you already believe. So, if you are not truly ready and open to this truth, and firmly committed to making a change, you won't be getting the meat out of this message any more than you've been able to accept it on previous occasions.

Your, "I already know this" filter

Acceptance of this truth gives you awe-inspiring manifesting powers. But before we expound on that, let's look at the powerful reality filter of those who will read this, thinking they already know this truth—I mean those who have already accepted an indwelling God as the basis for their religion.

2-To God or As God

One of the strange things about knowing a truth as powerful as—*God, as man, in man, is man*—is that your acceptance of this truth, in and of itself, can not change the quality of your life. This is because, even though you've embraced the idea on an intellectual level, your ego mind will still have a reality filter in place that keeps you penniless and powerless.
--The Science of Mind Textbook, -- Ernest Holmes

That's not to say you are actually penniless and powerless. But the point is; no matter what your situation or circumstances, you will be handicapped by a reality filter that's keeping you poorer in some way than you've wanted. We all have a reality filter in place.

The Belief System trap

And one of the strangest ways your reality filter can work is when you think you truly know something, when you only understand it at an intellectual level. This would be the case when you feel certain you know a truth, but have not yet proven it to yourself through demonstrated results.

For instance: your belief in an indwelling God can only be a theory for you, until you've proven it to yourself—until you've embodied that truth by being and becoming someone who has consciously and knowingly used this God power in manifesting your desires come true.

If you already believe in the reality of "God in man, is man" you might want to consider the fact that what you think you know about what you don't know is your greatest barrier to further spiritual enlightenment. What I'm offering you here is the spiritual path to a quality of life you've never known.

Your greatest barrier to acquiring this "pearl of great value" will be your assumed attitude of, *I already know this.* So hear this: if you are not already truly enjoying life, healthy, happy, and prosperous beyond your wildest dreams, you may think you know this truth, but you really didn't get it!

Believe me. As an individualization of God, your manifesting powers are truly awesome. If you are not there already, you might want to assume that something in your current Belief System stands between you and your ability to manifest as a god. Your Belief System is your reality concept filter.

In case you haven't noticed, **B**elief **S**ystem, when abbreviated, reads, **B.S.**

When you think you know

Strange as it may seem, those who think they already know this truth will be the least likely to get the message here. Those who have accepted the reality of an indwelling God as the basis of their religious belief may miss the life-changing message in this book. Why is that?

It is next to impossible to teach anyone something they think they already know. And if what we think we know about this indwelling essence of our being has boiled down into an intellectual understanding, we'll feel good, simply because we think we know the truth, when all we have is a belief.

Your manifesting powers come with a knowing that goes far beyond believing.

God doesn't fit in a box

The problem with intellectualizing God is that, in so doing, you've tried to take the essence of God and conceptualize it. That's like trying to put God or Spirit in a box (a reality concept). God, described, is no longer God.

God is not a thought, an idea, or an understanding. In fact, you might say God is pure Presence in the absence of thought. God is not a concept or a point of view. It is not even an experience. But you might say God is the pure essence behind the experience.

"Being" and "God," synonymous

To get a better feel for being present, think of the power of God in you as your expression of the "BEING Principle", and then see if you can accept the word "Being" and "God" as synonymous.

Play with that thought for a minute, and then ask yourself, who you would be being if you were being totally present-- just BEING in the absence of thought? See if you can say *I am* without adding anything after it. See if you can experience just "Being" –present without thought.

I hope this helps you see that in conceptualizing God, you've lost the essence of It. And your concept of God will stand between you and the experience of It.

Once you've locked into any belief, your reality filter will not allow you to hear or to accept even a different version of the same truth. The problem, here, is that an intellectual understanding about the true nature of your BEING is that God does not fit in that box or any other box.

To God or as God

On occasions when I've presented the Sunday message in a Science of Mind or a Unity church, I've asked the congregation this loaded question, *When you pray, do you pray to God or as God?* And each time, with the exception of a few knowing smiles, I see a room full of puzzled looks.

To God or As God

Prior to my asking this question, everyone in the room will have enthusiastically responded by raising their hand to the question, *Do you believe 'God as man, in man, is man?'* Their raised hands said they truly and passionately believe they are individualizations of God, and yet, my question about praying as God confounds them.

I find their response very interesting, especially considering the fact that the founder of Science of Mind, Ernest Homes said, *We can know God only so far as we can become God!* In that same paragraph, Holmes went on to say, *We partake of the Divine Nature, and the Universal personifies Itself through man in varying degrees, according to man's receptivity to it.*
The Science of Mind Textbook, -- Ernest Holmes

I'm not saying Holmes would have agreed with my version of this truth. It doesn't matter, one way or the other. The question is, **what do you think and how do you feel about the idea of praying as God?** So, think about it. If you truly believe *God as man, in man, is man,* then you are an individualization of God. And if that's true for you, then, the only way you can pray is AS GOD.

Think about that and let it sink in, and then ask yourself how much more powerful your prayers would be if you knew you were praying as a god rather than to God?

And now, let me ask you another question. *What if all your thoughts were powerful prayers, and what if all your prayers were answered?* Think about that for a moment and you'll be ready for the next chapter.

Chapter review

The power of God in you shows up as the BEING Principle—
that's the power you have to create a happier more
successful reality by simply choosing a new way of BEING
YOU. And you've been doing that all your life, (making new
being choices), but maybe this awesome power to BE is not
serving you with awe-inspiring manifestations.

If that's so, it's because you've forgotten you are an
individualization of God and that you have the power to
choose again and create a whole new reality.

You also seem not to know that you will automatically attract
whoever and whatever belongs with your new being choice.
But even so, it's working right now, attracting whatever
belongs in your life.

You have the power to create any new reality you can dream
up and it will manifest, as if by magic. You have the power to
make the quantum leap out of poverty and into riches, just
by choosing it, and the Universe must deliver on that BEING
choice.

Unfortunately, you have amnesia. You've forgotten you have
that power. It is the intention of this book that you find that
power and learn how to be a powerful manifestor.

All your prayers are answered

When Joe prays, *I'm poor, God; please, make me rich,* that prayer will be answered, because all our prayers are answered, believe it or not. But the answer won't be what Joe hoped for, nor will the answer come in the way you or Joe may have thought prayers were answered.

Because you are an individualization of God, you have undiscovered and untapped god-like powers. In fact, you have the power to answer your own prayers, and you're already doing that, conscious of it or not!

It is not necessary that you believe this in order to have it work for you; the power is there, functioning, manifesting results, whether you believe you have the power or believe you don't. So, how powerful would you be if you truly understood that power and had learned how to use it to your advantage on a daily basis?

How Prayers Get Answered

Of course, it wouldn't surprise me if you were shaking your head "NO" in disbelief. If you're having a hard time believing you are that powerful, that's okay. Read on, and you may change your mind.

If you're not already rich in health, wealth and/or relationships, it would be easy for you to make a case, proving your powerlessness, by simply pointing at the solid evidence—your life and your less-than-ideal circumstances.

For instance, maybe you're seeing the shaky condition of your finances as proof that you lack the power to change anything. Maybe your health is bad, or you have serious relationships problems. Any one of the above situations could have you feeling powerless. But let's see if we can shed a different sort of light on that solid evidence.

It would only be natural that you'd see your unpaid bills, as the cause of your financial dilemma, but what if your insufficient income were the effect, not the cause of your financial problems?

- o What if your focus on not having enough money to pay those bills were a creative force manifesting more of the same?
- o What if your focus on the problem of being in poor health were causing more poor health
- o What if your attention to the problems in your relationship were the causal force perpetuating that problem?

I know your ego mind doesn't want you to hear that, but that's exactly what's happening! Here's how it works; what you believe and how you feel about life creates your reality. And that reality concept is the model the Universe must use in filling the mold you've created with your being choice.

So, what is a BEING choice?

Once you've changed your attitude, your point of view or your opinion about anything, you've made a BEING choice. The Law of Attraction, set in motion by your new BEING commitment, then, brings into your life, a reality experience that must be a perfect match for your newest point of view about life.

As gods, individualized, we've each created our own reality, using powers we never even imagined we had. Because we have this built-in power to BE, every thought we think and every word we speak is a prayer, and all our prayers are answered. And it all happens automatically.

That's a little scary, when you stop to think about it, because some of your manifested results are not all that great—not at all what you wanted, are they?

- So, when you say something like, *I'm sick and tired of hearing you complain,* the answer to that prayer is, guess what—the experience of being sick and tired. Oops!

- When you say, *I hate my job,* you are actually saying *I am someone who hates his or her job.* In essence, you've just set yourself up (prayed) to have more reasons for not liking your job. Uh oh!

- When you keep asking yourself, w*hy the money always runs out before the end of the month,* you've said in effect, *I am someone who will never have enough money.* You've just prayed that you will never be rich! Oh no!

Once you've begun to realize that you're shooting yourself in the foot with that kind of thinking (praying), you'll begin paying closer attention to your thoughts. Since we become what we think about, and automatically attract whatever belongs with that way of thinking, you'll want to choose a whole new focus for your thoughts, won't you?

You're not really in charge of your thoughts, you know—at least not yet! Your ego mind is in charge, and that's why you keep focusing on what you don't want—praying for more of the same.

So, in taking charge, you might want to begin with the realization that all your thoughts are BEING choices. What!? You don't agree? Sorry, my friend, they are. Every attitude, opinion, and point of view you take on is a BEING choice.

Even simple preferences are, in fact, BEING choices.
- Choosing what you like and do not like, is a BEING choice.
- When you declare your favorite desert to be cherry pie, ala mode, you've chosen who you will BE relative to cherry pie and vanilla ice cream.
- Every time you think and every time you open your mouth to speak, you ARE choosing who you will be.

All your thoughts and words are, therefore, far more powerful and productive than you have allowed yourself to see. Just by thinking a thought or speaking your word, those two powerful principles are set in motion and must (by law) manifest the corresponding reality.

Why are our thoughts so powerful?
God experiences life in and through us as us. That's why we become what we think about; it's also why God hears our

prayers before they are spoken; it's because He individualized Himself in each of us.

That's what Christ meant when he said, *I and my Father are one, and ye are my brethren.*

If you're wondering why God doesn't step in automatically to solve our problems when we get in trouble; it's because His love for us is unconditional. He lovingly put a part of Himself in each of us, giving us the power of choice—the power to choose who we would be.

His solemn promise, along with that awesome gift of Self, is to not to interfere with our choices. His unconditional love has created the space for us to grow and learn from our own mistakes.

So for as long as we continue to make the same dumb BEING decisions, over and over again, we'll automatically suffer the same undesirable consequences that, just naturally, belong with that BEING choice.

But then there's the other side of that same coin. When we wake up and start making wiser BEING choices, we'll reap the corresponding awesome benefits—and I do mean, awesome!

So, what's the purpose of it all?
Our job in the Game of Life, as individualizations of God, is to grow our consciousness; that means we will gradually become more and more aware of our True Identity. To encourage our further growth in consciousness, we are occasionally urged and sometimes inspired to make out-of-

the-box BEING choices—and get this—with the guarantee that our prayer will be answered!

Once we've tested and proven our manifesting powers to ourselves and have accepted this profound truth of our BEING as what's so for us, we'll have the world by the tail. We'll be choosing one daring out-of-the-box adventure after another. The more you believe in yourself, the more powerful you'll become and the more spectacular the results!

Until then—until we've truly found our power and taken charge of our thoughts—the majority of humanity will choose to run and hide from this truth. That's because most of us live our lives as our egos. And your ego is afraid that you will discover just how powerful you really are!

Our survival oriented egos, playing it safe, will continue to deny us the good life, because it fears what's outside the box.

To exemplify our fear of the unknown, I'm reminded of the Latin American General who tested the courage of political prisoners by giving them two fearful options. They could either fight the hungry lion in the pit or take their chances with unknown dangers that could lurk behind the black door.

And which option—the lion, or the black door—do you suppose the majority of those political prisoners chose? Which one would you choose? It is reported that the majority of his prisoners chose to fight a hungry lion in the pit rather than face the unknown dangers they imagined might be hiding behind the black door.

So, what was actually behind that black door? The general obviously had a sense of humor. There was nothing but freedom behind that black door. And, that's what's behind your black door—the freedom to be YOU in a brand new way!

Let's face it; if you're stuck in the status-quo, it is because you'd rather put up with those undesirable circumstance than face the unknown reality outside your box.

The truth is, once you've faced your fears, you'll be free to experience life in a grand new way and you'll automatically reap the good life outside that box.

So, here's a question for you: Are you sufficiently fed up with being powerless—fed up with feeling like the victim of your circumstances? Are you ready yet to choose your way out of that box and BE you in a spanking new way?

The only way out is through, and the way out begins with a reality check. It begins by your taking a long hard look at your circumstances, and being willing to admit that you're not too happy with the way things turned out.

Notice that no problem is ever solved, until you've first admitted to yourself that you DO, in fact, have a problem. So, first acknowledge the existence of your problem, and then take responsibility for having created it.

How did you create the problem? You did that with an unwise BEING choice. That's right; you created the reality in which that problem persists. So don't expect to get at the real truth about the way things are if you'd be taking inventory through the eyes of a victim.

If you are seeing yourself as a victim of your circumstances, the victim's attitude in you will not allow you to learn the truth. So, if your ego has assumed the role of victim, you'll need to take over the controls. In order to do a reality check, the Real You must supervise the inventory taking.

Then, once you've taken a serious look at your current circumstances and found them lacking, you'll want to accept full responsibility for having created the reality in which those undesirable conditions are now the standard.

Believe me, continued attachment to that poor-me attitude will only get you more reasons to feel like a victim.

But once you've realized that you've created that mess with an unwise BEING choice—in that moment of revelation— you will have regained your power of choice. You will know, in that "ah ha" moment, that you have what it takes to re-choose your way out of the problem.

What we're looking for in doing this reality check is a motivational spur—a powerful reason for choosing out of your box into far better circumstances.

To effect that change of circumstances, it will be necessary that you change your mind about who you are—and that, my friend is a transformation in consciousness, and it is the only way out of your box. Once you've chosen, you will have been transformed, as the apostle, Paul said,

...by the renewing of your mind

Now, if you're still laboring under the common misconception that your fate is set in concrete, and your unhappy circumstances are merely God's way of punishing you for your sins, you'll want to read the next chapter about the will of God before you move on to a life filled with better things.

4. The Will of God

HAVE
DO SUCCESS
BE STAIRWAY

The Will of God may seem a strange subject for this book, but believe me it isn't. There are a great many people on this planet Earth who are poor, because they believe making a great deal of money would be contrary to God's will for us.

And, of course, I beg to differ with that point of view—that money is evil, and rich people are the bad guys--; that's why this is an appropriate subject for this book.

One of our purposes in discussing the Will of God here is to assist you in replacing some of your old subconscious notions about the evils of becoming wealthy. The truth is, God actually wants you to become wealthy, if that is your desire. Knowing that should allow you to really feel good about the idea of becoming exceptionally wealthy.

Anti-rich propaganda

My bet is that some anti-rich propaganda you learned, maybe in Sunday school—that poverty is next to Godliness is a belief still hidden somewhere in your subconscious. That hidden agenda would have you feeling guilty about wanting lots of money. Throw that idea out with the garbage.

What half truths were you taught about money as *the root of all evil* by a well-meaning Sunday school teacher that now needs to be erased from your programming?

What is the will of God for you on the subject of becoming rich in all ways? What does God will for you? Have you ever allowed yourself to consider that question, maybe thinking outside the box of your previous religious beliefs?

What is God's plan for you?

From previous chapters you have learned and hopefully accepted that you are an individualization of God. What do YOU suppose God intends for you and me? Does He even have an intention, a plan?

Is there a purpose to life that, once discovered, will show us the way to *...thy kingdom come; thy will be done*? And if there's a hidden purpose, what is it, exactly? What are God's intentions for you?

Get serious about finding your own answer for that question. Whatever you come up with, will inspire and empower you to take your own quantum leap of faith. Your answer to that question could inspire you to write your mission statement. And, believe me, those who know their true purpose in life are the most inspired and powerful people on the planet.

So, take a moment to ponder the question, *What's God's plan for me?* Don't take my word for it; see if you can come up with an answer for yourself. Your tendency will be to rely on what you've always believed about 'the will of God, but don't go there; try a new approach to the question.

Every religion on earth was established by someone who thought he had the only right answer to that question. In his quest for the truth, he found God in his heart, but when he tried to explain what he'd gotten, words failed him and the true essence of God would have been lost in translation.

The point being that in order to truly know God, we can't really take someone else's word for it; we must each have and experience our own relationship to God.

So, based on any new awareness you may have acquired while reading this book, what would you suppose is God's plan for you? What does God will for you? What would you guess? ...or maybe you're waiting for God's instructions?

I'm waiting for God to tell me

At a minister's conference, a few years ago, one minister after another stood to share their intention for their ministries for the next year. One of those ministers said, *I don't have a plan; I'm waiting for God to tell me what to do.* Unless that minister finally woke up to the fact that God won't be telling him what to do with his life, he's still waiting for an answer.

In the Lord's Prayer, the words, *thy will be done* always bothered me because "will power," for me, was a grit your teeth and make it happen sort of a power. As a kid I had a great deal of what I called, "will power," but back then, I was coming from the point of view, *"If it is to be, it's up to me."*

My living example of what 'thy will be done' meant was my Father's, *Obey my rules or be punished.* And since I didn't believe God would be ordering me around, punishing me if I broke the rules, I couldn't buy into the Lord's Prayer. My Sunday school student's opinion about *the will of God* back then was that it didn't make sense, because a loving God would not be willing me to do anything.

The power of will

When I was 15, I read a book titled, Power of Will, by Frank Channing Haddock. What I thought I read in that book, back then, seemed to confirm what I already believed about the power of will—that it was a make-it-happen sort of power.

In researching this chapter, I looked for that book to confirm my *'I already know this'* definition of "will power." What I found in that book surprised me with an entirely different definition for will power than I had led myself to believe all those years. The definition for "will power" in that book is, *The Soul Itself, Exercising Self-direction.*

And then I checked the dictionary and found this definition, *the drive to perfect and transcend the self through the possession and exercise of creative power.*

Wow! Isn't that what I've been teaching you –that you'll be transformed once you've chosen out of your box into a new way of exercising your creative powers—you'll transcend the old you with a new way of BEING you.

So, with the idea in mind, that God individualized Himself in each of us, take another look at your question about the will of God for you. Here's my answer: God individualized Himself in each of us, and then set us free to discover this as our True Identity. Our mission in life, (God's will for us), is that we discover the power of God in us by consciously using that power to create whatever reality we can dream up. That's why we were given imaginations.

The God power in us

The BEING Principle, is exercised when we choose a new way of being. As each new BEING choice is manifested by the Law of Attraction, we become more consciously aware of our growing power to BE more than we were.

So know this: if you're waiting for God to tell you what to do, He won't. He gave you the power of choice; it's up to you to discover that power and learn how to use it wisely. You'll learn only by choosing—through trial and error. The more choices you make, the faster you'll learn your true identity.

You want help from God? It will come to you in two forms:
o   Divine Discontent
o   And Inspiration

If you become too attached and comfortable with the status quo, God will make your feather bed uncomfortable. This nudge from God is called, *Divine Discontent*. When coasting, as in, *"I've got it made in the shade,"* God will probably move the shade. That's your message from God, that it's time to move onward and upward in consciousness.

God's help comes to us in the form of inspiration. The word inspire, means "breath life into." That new aliveness in us comes into being once we've made a new being commitment. In that moment when you feel inspired to make your next move out of the box, that inspiration is God 'breathing life into your idea.'

The Will of God

Thy will be done

- The will of God is that you exercise the BEING Principle, consciously creating your own reality.
- The will of God is that you continue to grow in consciousness—becoming more consciously aware that your true identity is spirit.

Your true mission in life is self-discovery. You are powerful beyond your wildest dream. Your job is to discover that power by using it, consciously, to manifest your magnificent obsession. The trick is to not become attached to those manifested results.

Thy kingdom come

Thy kingdom come is a place of bliss, peace, joy, and happiness. You'll seek those four heart felt conditions as the hoped-for result of acquiring some form of material benefit.

And then one fine day, when you've mastered the art of applying the BEING Principle as the solution for all your health, wealth and relationship problems, you'll realize that *thy kingdom come* was there all the while waiting for your BEING choice.

Bliss, peace, joy and happiness are simply BEING choices. What would your life be like if you went for the joy instead of the stuff you think you'd enjoy if you had it?

The will of God is that you be a god, the creator of your own reality. The will of God is that you finally come to know God. And to know God you must practice at being god in all aspects of your life.

But before you make your next move and choose out of that box, you might want to read the next chapter and learn the hidden secret to winning big at the Game of Life.

Acquiring the winner's attitude

Have you ever noticed that those who win big at the Game of Life play the game as if they had nothing to loose? The big winners in life have no fear of losing. In fact, that's the real secret to their winning:

> *Before you can win at anything,*
> *you must first give up your fear of losing.*

In other words, *you'll never win what you can't afford to loose.* If you feel you can't afford to lose a bet you just made, you will lose it. You can't bet the rent money and win!

Let me repeat the rule—you might want to write it on a 3x5 card and put it where you'll see it every day, until you've acquired the winner's attitude. The rule is:

You cannot win what you can't afford to lose.

Why is that so? If you think you can't afford to loose, you'll be afraid of loosing, and you'll be motivated by fear. Can fear ever win the day for you? Can you win if you are afraid you'll lose? Never! Why is that?

Once you're afraid, you'll lack the winner's attitude, and without it, you can't win. So, what does it take to win? It takes courage and a winning attitude to win.

A transformation from loser to winner

Alice called me, one day, out of the blue, and introduced herself as a visitor to my BEING Workshop website. Alice asked,

> *Does this stuff really work?*

And I replied with,

> *What stuff, Alice? To what stuff are you referring?*

Alice rephrased the question,

> *The BEING Solution—does it really work?*

And I responded with,

> *Yes, the BEING Solution is a principle and principles always work. But you'll get the results you want only after you've applied the BEING principle as the solution to your problem.*
> *So, Alice, what's your problem?*

And then Alice shared her predicament with me, She said,

> *I own a $1,200,000 house with an $800,000 mortgage on it, and I'm 3 months behind in the mortgage payments. I'm afraid I'm going to lose it all. Can you help me?*

My answer:

> *Alice, let me send you free, the first four chapters of BEING THE SOLUTION. If you are inspired by what you've read there, call me again, and we'll talk about the BEING Workshop.*

Six months later, after completing her third time through the workshop, I questioned Alice about the state of her finances. I asked,

> *When you called me six months ago, Alice, you were about to lose your million-dollar+ home, and you asked me, 'Does this stuff really work?' So, tell me, Alice, what do you think? Did the BEING Solution really work for you? And if so, what is the current state of your finances?*

Alice answered,

> *Yes, it really does work! In fact, it's a little hard for me to believe the answer to my financial problems could have been that simple.*

> *Not only did I solve my money problems, I'm a totally different person now than before the workshop. And the best part of that change in me is in how my relationship with my husband and kids has changed for the better.*

> *I took the workshop three times and had a new transformation each time. Today, after the third time through, I have a net worth of 14 million dollars and a positive cash flow of $18,000 a month.*

Of course, Alice is not her real name, but this is a true story. Let's hope it inspires you to take a walk through YOUR OWN BLACK DOOR, out of your problem reality, and into a life of prosperous living!

Giving up the fear

I talked to Alice right after she'd read the first four chapters of BEING THE SOLUTION. The first thing I asked was,
Alice, can you make it okay to lose the house?

All Alice needed, in order to turn her life and her finances around was a winning attitude. And for as long as she remained deathly afraid of losing the house, she would not have a winner's attitude, and therefore, would not have the attitude necessary for solving her money problems.

I pointed out to Alice, that for as long as she continued to focus all her attention on the problem, she would never, ever manifest a solution. Of course, Alice had the usual and natural reaction to my suggestion and responded with,

> *There's no way I can make that okay!*

But after we talked for a while, Alice realized that letting go of the house is what she had to do—get past her fear of losing it. So she imagined the worst possible outcome—the dire consequences of that happening, and made that okay.

As soon as Alice made it okay to lose the house, the fear was gone. And that's when the light dawned!

Then Alice was able to make a new BEING choice to, once again, BE the successful person she had been, before her cash flow turned negative and the fear took over. In that moment of freedom from fear, when Alice made losing the house okay, her winning attitude returned.

In each of the three BEING workshops in which Alice participated, she was further transformed, and with each transformation, her courage, confidence and self-worth grew.

What's a transformation? It is what happens in that moment when you've changed your mind about who you are. It's what happens, when suddenly; you acquire that can-do attitude and are no longer afraid.

It is in that moment of revelation when you rediscover your power of choice. Then, once you've made your new BEING choice, the automatic prayer-answering process clicks in to manifest whatever belongs in your new reality.

As an individualization of God, one would assume one's life would be wonderful, but it isn't, is it? So what's standing between you and wonderful? What's keeping you poorer than you've wanted to be? You'll need to know the answer to that question, before you attempt to apply what you've learned, so far.

So, is fear a bad thing?
If you've chosen a goal since you started reading this book, I'm sure you've also experienced some fears popping up around that choice. So does that mean fear is a bad thing?

Don't label your fears good or bad. Fear is an important element in your ability to survive. Fear is your ego mind's early warning signal; it is your built-in survival system at work, warning you of some perceived danger.

That's the good news

But your ego mind will see every proposed change of attitude, point of view, or circumstances as a threat to its survival. For your ego to keep you safe, the status quo must remain in tact. So, some dangers will be very real, but most of what you fear will be a product of your ego's over-active imagination. In most cases, the danger will seem real, even though it is not.

Unfortunately, your fears have great manifesting powers. Whatever you choose to believe must become your experience—your manifested reality. It's the law! Your fears are simply negative faith in the process of manifesting what you don't want; so if you are ever to win big in the Game of Life, you must first conquer your fear of losing.

An eight-step process for dealing with your fear

Your first step out of fear would be to notice that only your ego is afraid; the 'Real You' encourages life out of that box. To deal with your ego's fears, you'll want to begin by:
1. Noticing that your ego (not the Real You) is afraid.
2. Then make it totally okay that you, as your ego, are afraid.
3. But you are not your ego, so talk to it and thank your ego for warning you about a possible danger.

Once the Real You has acknowledged the presence of fear, analyze the perceived threat and do one of two things:
4. decide how you will deal with any real danger,
5. or smile, and dismiss any false danger signals.

Most ego fears are based on some unreal, imagined danger. As the saying goes; **'FEAR,'** is merely, False Evidence Appearing Real. So, whenever the fear shows up, ask yourself, *Is this threat for real or is it imagined?*

If the perceived danger is real—(a possible outcome of your current situation),

6. Picture the worst possible conclusion and all its possible repercussions.
7. Then allow yourself to imagine that the worst has already happened. *DELAY*

See if you can allow yourself to experience exactly how you would feel if the worst case scenario had already happened. Compare this to how you'd feel if you had already jumped off the high diving board into the deep water; you've just touched bottom; now what do you do?

I want you to see that once you've touched bottom, in any situation, you've reached that low point where there's nowhere to go, but up. And once you see that your only choice out of the pits is up, then, and only then, will you make an inspired decision.

8. Now that you've faced your fear, and accepted the worst possible outcome, you'll make that inspired decision. Notice that the worst hasn't really happened, so you still have time to save the day with an inspired decision to act.

In the deep water, you'll bend your knees and spring off the bottom with renewed energy and enthusiasm. Notice once you are looking up, you'll see the light and the fear is gone!

To review what we've just covered

In solving any problem, your worst enemy, the powerful paralyzer, will be your fear of failure. So, to take charge of your fears,

1. Allow yourself to experience your fears full out, and the worst possible scenario.
2. Make the fear okay.

3. Accept the possibility of failure.
4. Then take your attitude out of the mud and into the stars.
5. Recreate that winning attitude.

What is a winner's attitude?

A winner's attitude is more than a state of mind; it is actually a spiritual awakening that allows you to know, intuitively, that you'll win no matter what obstacles you may face along the way toward your goal.

It is that Spirit of Aliveness in you that will step into and fill the gap once your fear has gone away. In that moment of making it totally okay to fail, you will have experienced your ego's death and rebirth.

Some other ways to describe a winner's attitude,
- o Self-confidence
- o Increased self-worth
- o Freedom from doubt
- o Belief in one's self and one's abilities
- o Certainty
- o Authority.

You could call it all of the above, but it's really much more than that—it's the Real You in charge!

Why does having the winner's attitude make you a certain winner?

To really understand the awesome power in a winner's attitude, you must realize that belief in one's self and belief in God are synonymous. Think about that truth for a moment and allow it to really sink in. Given that you are an individualization of God, self-confidence is actually the most powerful form of riches on the planet.

To God or As God

So, once you've acquired certainty, that knowing feeling, that can't-lose attitude, you will have become, in that inspired moment, one with God, and as such cannot fail, no matter what you attempt.

You might want to read that again, because once you've acquired certainty, you've found the power behind your ability to manifest at will!.

If the idea of being one with God rattles your religious beliefs, you might want to remember that Christ said,
I and my father are one, and ye are my brethren.

Once you've conquered your fear of failure and have the winner's attitude the Real You is in charge and that makes you invincible.

So, once again, how does one acquire a winner's attitude?

- o It begins with making it okay to fail,
- o and then in having the courage (Spirit) to do what you feared doing
- o You'll grow more confident with each successful venture outside the box, so--
- o Be willing to learn from your mistakes
- o Keep on doing it, until you get it right
- o With each success you'll acquire more of the winner's attitude—that sense of certainty that allows you to know you can't fail.

A glass cutter's nightmare

As a Corporal Technician in A Company, 373 Engineers Division, US Army, during WWII, I had been assigned the task of repairing and replacing broken windows and glass in a bombed-out French fort in LeHavre, France. My work crew consisted of 40 French carpenters. The fort was to be a debarkation station for US soldiers who had completed tours of duty.

My assignment, in addition to that of supervising the French carpenters was to cut the glass for those broken windows. These were hand-made wooden windows with fan-shaped panes at the top. All glass sizes were non-standard and each fan-shaped pane would be cut to the shape of a paper pattern brought to me by the French carpenters.

Prior to the war, as a carpenter, I occasionally cut glass and considered myself an expert. I had been put in charge of that operation, because I volunteered my skills as a glass cutter. But my first attempt at cutting French glass turned out to be a miserable disaster.

At first, I thought something was wrong with the French glass—maybe it was too brittle. And even though I blamed the glass, my confidence dwindled somewhat.

The French carpenter, who brought me the paper pattern, smiled at my failed attempt and shook his head in disgust. His critical look said, "This dumb American soldier doesn't know what the hell he's doing."

But I thought, "I AM an expert at cutting glass," so I regained my composure and tried again. This time the result was the same, but now I had an audience of two judgmental French carpenters. Their pained looks of disapproval were telling me I should turn the job over to one of them. In fact, one of them volunteered, but I stubbornly refused.

I broke many more pieces of glass that morning—I have no clear idea how many. And as my audience of disparaging

French carpenters continued to grow, so did my frustration and embarrassment. They were obviously appalled as they watched this apparently unskilled American soldier wasting precious glass in war-time France.

My aggravation and upset grew, until I finally reached a breaking point. In that turn-around moment, I just didn't care or give a damn how many pieces of glass I broke. That's when the miracle happened. From that moment on, every cut was picture perfect.

In that moment of not caring, I went from a loser's attitude to a winner's attitude. What actually happened here? In that moment of careless abandon I had just made it totally okay to fail. I had become a certain winner, because I was no longer afraid to fail.

And, that's the secret to acquiring the winner's attitude! The trick to winning is:

*Before you can win at anything,
you must first make it okay to loose!*

That's easier said than done, but it's totally necessary to make it okay to loose if you sincerely want to win.

Mistakes—the foundation for your success

In the process of acquiring the winner's attitude, you'll want to learn to view a failure as nothing more serious than a learning experience. So, have you made failure your friend?

Your ability to see failure as a mere stepping stone on your way to success, is a very powerful remedy for your fears.

The Winner's Attitude

Starting from scratch, in 1949, with only $2000 of my own money to invest I created an incredibly successful business with over 100 employees. I had no business education except while selling newspapers as a kid. So, I had to learn how to run a successful business the hard way.

Looking back at my success, I've realized that 70% of my original decisions were wrong. But I learned from each of those mistakes, and each time chose again. My formula for success was simple.
Keep doing what works and stop doing what doesn't work.

Think about this and see if you can get this lesson of life:
—my mistakes were the foundation for my success.

The, Ready, Fire, Aim success strategy
My winning success strategy has always been, *Ready, Fire Aim.* I've always made quick, result oriented decisions. If one of my doing choices didn't produce the intended results, I chose again. Why am I telling you this story?

If you can continue making out-of-the-box BEING choices, welcoming failure as your best friend, using Ready-Fire-Aim as your success strategy, you will succeed at whatever you attempt, no matter what path in life you take.

But you do have a success barrier
If you've tried and failed, before, it's because a part of you fears success more than failure. In the next chapter, you'll learn what's stopping you—what stands between you and the success you've always wanted.

The Brick Wall

Your Success Barriers

What's stopping you

You have the power, as an individualization of God, to make a new BEING choice—to take the quantum leap—that would transform the quality of your life forever. You could do that right now; you could take a leap of faith out of those undesirable circumstances and into the reality of happiness, joy and prosperity.

You could have already done that, but you haven't. Do you know why not?

As soon as you've committed to a new way of BEING you, the Universe will be making delivery; it is truly primed, ready and waiting for your new BEING choice. So when will you find the courage to go for it and choose the good life for yourself? What are you waiting for?

Think about it! You could be having whatever you want from life, just by choosing it! Life really is that simple! Even your bible tells you, *Seek and ye shall find. Ask and it shall be given.* So what's stopping you?

What's Stopping You?

Why aren't you already rich in love, health, wealth and relationships?

In the first five chapters, I've made the solving of life's problems sound simple and easy. And it really is that simple. The solution to your worst problem is nothing more complicated than a new BEING choice. But why can't you choose? What stands between you and having life be that great?

The problem is, you've already chosen

When you were a kid, you came to some erroneous conclusion about life; you made up your mind as a 4 year old that you were not good enough, smart enough or big enough and maybe that you were worthless and unlovable. None of that was really true, but you've been accumulating evidence to prove that 4-year-old's perspective on life ever since.

Allow yourself to see that your reality concept is no more than an illusion. It's just your story about life—a story you made up as you went along, and it's not for real. But that story has become your act, and you've been running your act, acting out a role in an ever repeating story, ever since.

So, you've spent your whole life, up until now trying to prove you were good enough, loveable and worth something or that you weren't. You might want to notice that whatever you were trying to prove didn't really need proving.

So, all this time, you've been a Don Quixote fighting a windmill. You chose your battle, your windmill, when you were just a child. You decided, back then, that there was

something you needed to prove, and now, for as long as you keep running your act, you'll still be trying to prove it.

You were always good enough
The joke is that you were always good enough, smart enough, and loveable if you could only have accepted that as your reality. So, your windmill was a figment of a 4-year old's reality concept. But that child's fairy tale will still be running your life, until you no longer feel the need to prove what didn't need proving in the first place.

Your current circumstances are real enough, but they've shown up in your life because they belong in the reality of your current **Belief System**. You may not like what's shown up, but the Universe has merely delivered content, conditions and circumstances that just naturally belong with that reality concept.

Once you've changed your mind about anything, you've taken on a new point of view, and as a result, you can expect a corresponding set of circumstances to soon follow. But, the reverse is also true. For as long as you maintain a self-limiting perspective on life, you'll remain stuck in that box, with those circumstances.

Your black door
Remember the story about the political prisoners who would rather face a hungry lion in the pit than deal with the fearful unknown outside the black door? You also have a black door you are afraid to walk through.

You live in a self-built box, (we all do) and you're stuck in that reality concept with those circumstances, because you're afraid of the unknown outside that box. That's YOUR black door. And unless you are far above the average, your

fear of what might or might not happen, if you ventured outside your current reality, will have you stopped dead in your tracks. The average person is so thoroughly attached to the role of a victim, he or she wouldn't consider choosing out and into more rewarding circumstances.

That's because, choosing out of the victim's role would mean sacrificing his or her identity.

What exactly is a victim story?

As an individualization of God, you are the creator of your own experience. The god part of you doesn't make excuses; so, any attempt to explain why your life isn't working will be a victim story.

Everyone has a tale of woe. You've got one too; it's whatever excuse you use to explain why your life didn't turn out the way you wanted. You may want to accept that your excuse is just a story, pure fiction, and you made it up.

But, your fairy tale about why your life isn't perfect is a very deep trap. The only way out of that pity party is to take full responsibility for having created the reality in which those victim's circumstances must continue to prevail.

Your reality concept, your victim story, is who you are, and any attempt to change your self-concept or your point of view about life will create an identity crisis for your ego.

Only by taking responsibility for your creation will you find your way out of that trap. Stepping out of your victim's role will also free and empower you in a way you'd never even imagined could happen.

What is ego?

Ego is the change-resistant part of you, the actor in your play, acting out the role you've chosen to play. Ego is the means by which you, as spirit, express life in a material reality.

Ego is your survival mechanism keeping you safe and out of harms way. When you hear that little voice in the back of your head telling you why you shouldn't, venture out of that box; that's your ego telling you life outside the box is not safe. That noise in your head is called mind chatter. Your ego fears change like you might fear death

Why do we have an ego?
Not only did God, as Spirit, put a part of Himself in each of us; He gave us egos so we, as spiritual beings, could experience life in a material reality.

As a truth seeker, you may have thought of yourself as a human being seeking a spiritual awakening. Actually, it's the other way around. As an individualization of God you are a spiritual being experiencing life in a material reality.

As Spirit, we require a material reality in which to express our creativity, and while in the BEING mode, we need an identity, a way in which to express our individuality, a way to relate to the people and things in our life. Your self-concept is you, BEING you in whatever way you've chosen to relate to life.

In any moment of now, you, as Spirit, can change your mind about who you will BE and how you will relate to life, but your ego doesn't see it that way. Ego doesn't see itself as just acting out the role you've chosen for it; your ego has accepted your reality concept as real, and it has taken on the identity of the character in the play you've written.

What's Stopping You?

As far as ego is concerned, that self concept is who you are, and any attempt to rewrite the script that runs your life, is a death sentence for your ego.

Ego's job in life is the survival of its being whoever it perceives itself to be. While in the survival mode, your ego cannot accept the idea of being reborn into the new reality as a good thing. So, expect your ego to resist any attempt to change reality concepts.

Your job, as the one in charge (spirit), is to rewrite the script of your play, and then to sell your ego on its new role in life. Selling your ego on the new reality may turn out to be a much bigger job than you have imagined.

The change you want will happen only after you've made it your empowered intention to take control and put the Real You in charge. Once Spirit, not ego, has the controls, you will have become "captain of your soul, master of your fate".

Your first step out of ego entrapment would be to remember that you are not your ego. Throughout the rest of this book I will be reminding you that your act is not who you really are. In order to stay on the same page with what you'll find in this book, you'll want to make it your mission to put Spirit, the Real You, more and more in charge. .

So, keep this in mind; you have an ego, but you are not your ego. You are, instead, an individualization of God, experiencing life in a material reality. Your ego is merely the means by which you've been able to materialize and experienced that reality concept as real.

Ego is your servant, not your master, but ego doesn't see it that way. So, anytime you're not paying strict attention, your ego will automatically take over control as master of the ship. Up until now, your ego has been the one in charge of your thinking 24/7. Spirit has been there, always, but in the background, constantly nudging you toward further growth in consciousness. But spirit has not taken charge, yet; so, ego has been, not so gleefully, running the show.

Only as spirit will you choose out

Each time you've ventured outside your box in the past, it was Spirit choosing out. But each time out (and there have been many times) there was a brief period of enthusiasm and joy, reveling in your new sense of aliveness, and then you grew careless, aimless and listless; that's the process for turning the controls over to your ego.

Notice that, with each success, you've merely created a larger sand box in which to play at the Game of Life. That's the story of your life and also the source of your problems in a nutshell. Even though you've bravely ventured out of your box from time to time, you've merely trapped yourself, each time, in a larger box.

Actually that's the way the Game of Life is played, the problem is that, for most of the game, your ego has been master of the ship. If you want your life and your *'freedom to BE'* back, you'll need to take over the controls. How do you do that?

You'll need a destination

The first thing you'll want to decide, as the new master, is your destination. No point in taking the wheel if you have no idea where the ship is going. So, your first step in taking charge of your life would be for you to choose a new reality, a new destination for your life and new way of BEING you.

What's Stopping You?

Are you ready to take your quantum leap of faith into a new reality of joy, happiness and prosperity? Then make it your intention to put the Real You in charge by choosing out of your old box.

Your ego will be deathly afraid of any reality concept change, so you can expect it to resist the change you want with all it's considerable might. Most people, who want life to get better, never make it past that initial ego resistance; so they stay trapped in the status quo for their whole lives.

If you really want out of that box to stay, you'll want to be powerfully motivated.

To find your way out to stay,
- You'll need a strong reason for wanting out of (escaping) the status quo.
- You must be clear about what you want instead—the new reality vision must be clear, exciting, and inspiring.
- You must truly believe the change you want is achievable.
- And you must want a change so bad you can taste it.
- And then, be committed to choosing it in spite of ego resistance.

But before you attempt your first step out of your box, let's look at how you built that reality concept cage and boxed yourself in with it.

You built a major part of that cage (your Belief System) before you were old enough and wise enough to think for yourself. You began creating those self-limiting beliefs (the bars of your cage) by buying into the opinions and prejudices of adults who, themselves, had bought someone else's opinion.

And that's how realities are built, out of attitudes, opinions and points of view. Think about it; those are pretty flimsy building materials, wouldn't you say!? You created your own individualized reality by simply choosing what to believe. And it matters not what you believe, the Universe will deliver content that must be a perfect match for that reality context.

You've created your own reality by choosing what to believe and your self-concept is the prime mover in maintaining that reality concept. That's your box, and you'll be stuck in it, until you're finally fed up with those circumstances and ready to choose out. How about now?

Are you ready to stop trying to prove to yourself that you're good enough or not, smart enough or not, loveable or not?

It should be abundantly clear to you by now, that if you truly desire a change in your life, you must, first, be willing to change your mind about who you are and what you believe! And to get a wiser perspective on your beliefs, let's label those ideas, "your **B**elief **S**ystem", the abbreviation of which is B.S. Be advised that your B.S. is a trap—an illusion!

Most people will never choose out of their boxes, because they have convinced themselves there's no way out. In fact, your ego's number one favorite trap is, "There is no way out", and it almost always works. Isn't that what's keeping you boxed in?

For as long as you continue to believe there's no way out, it would be pointless to even hope for life to get better. But, there IS a way out and it's called the quantum leap—a new BEING choice.

What's Stopping You?

To reaffirm your belief that there truly IS a way out, let's review the principles governing your life—The BEING Principle, and The Attraction Principle. The number one principle controlling your destiny is the BEING Principle—*we become what we think about.* If you want to take charge of your life, choose out of that box and take charge of your thinking.

Changing the pattern of your thinking changes who you are BEING, and, in case you'd forgotten, your new BEING choice becomes a powerful prayer that the Universe must bring into manifestation. It's the law that your reality concept must manifest!

The prayer answering process is, the Law of Attraction, responding automatically to bring into your life who and what belongs in the reality of that BEING commitment. You'll know for certain, that you've truly found a way out of those undesirable circumstances, when your belief in principle becomes unshakable.

But before you attempt the take over the controls, you might want to reflect on the idea that you've already become what you've thought about. All those old thoughts and ideas from your past have combined to form your self-concept and make you into you who you are now. You also might want to allow yourself to see that some of those thoughts were the illogical conclusions of a small unreasonable child--YOU.

Changing who you are BEING will require some major out-of-the-box thinking. Two things created your current box, setting the outer boundaries for your thinking.
   1. Your self concept
   2. Your reality concept

To God or As God

And for as long as you stay trapped in that old way of thinking, all your self-limiting thoughts will set the outer limits for what you may have in life. To change the content in your life you must begin by imagining what your life would be like if you were already enjoying the good life outside that box.

To make it past your ego's resistance to change, you'll need an even more powerful reason for coming out of your box. So, why do you want out of that box and how bad do you want out? … bad enough to choose out?

Before life can get better for you, you must
1. Believe it can happen
2. Want that change so bad you can taste it
3. Only then will you find the courage to choose out of your box.

What you don't like about your current situation could be the spur under your saddle and sufficient reason for escaping the status quo.

But get this: wanting out may get you out of your box, but it won't keep you out. For instance, hating that spare tire around your waist might have you choosing to loose weight, but you'll need a more inspiring reason than that; you'll need an empowered BEING commitment

If you want to lose the weight and keep it off, you'll need sustaining motivation, a vision of what your life would be like and feel like if you weighed 30 lbs. less. What would you look like; how would you feel about yourself? You'll want to imagine having more energy, enjoying life more, wearing nicer fitting clothes.

Once you've made that vision real, so exciting and compelling, you WILL take your quantum leap out of the old and into that new reality of you being 30 pounds lighter. You'll choose out once your vision becomes a BEING choice, and your desire turns into enthusiastic anticipation. At that point, you've chosen out of your box; now the trick is, to stay out.

Once you're out, your ego will have a whole different bag of tricks for getting you back into the old box. And, believe me your ego is good at its job. How good? You can bet anyone who is not already rich wants to be richer than they are now. Yet, according to an IRS report, about 85% of all US citizens will reach retirement age with insufficient income on which to retire and live at their current standard of living.

In other words, 85% will retire much poorer than they've wanted to be, even after they have chosen out of the old box. That's because their egos tricked them back into it. That means, only 15% of you will make it past that powerful ego resistance, unless of course you make the inspired BEING commitment that changes those odds.

So, let's assume you're reading this book because you want the quality of your life to change somehow. You may be inspired enough by what you've read so far that you'll choose that better life for yourself. Let's say you've finally made it out of your box. The hard part will be for you to stay out, once you've gotten out

The following chapters will help you understand your ego's resistance to change and give you a number of powerful tools for dealing with it. The intent of this book is to lead you down the path toward having the Real You take charge of your life.

Before we look at those tools, let's look at the story of your life, the story that has you trapped—your act.

7. Trapped In Your Act

You have an act—we all do. Here's how I created my act: As a four-year old, I followed my older brother to school one day. When he finally noticed, my brother became very angry with me and cursed at me all the way back home. *Damn you, you're making me late for school.*

As a kid, I worshiped my big brother, so his anger cut me to the core. While feeling hurt and resentful, I came to the erroneous conclusion that since my only real friend, my big brother, didn't love me anymore, nobody did. My way of dealing with that foolish conclusion was to decide, *To hell with them. I don't need anyone.*

That conclusion, "that nobody loved me," became the story that would run my life. My reactive decision that "I didn't need anyone," created my act (a way of BEING) that would hide the real me from the world--and also from myself.

Trapped in Your Act

I want you to see that this 4-year-old's foolish conclusion and his reactive decision about how to deal with life could not have been farther from the truth. But those non-truths would still run my life for over 40 years. Don't even think about feeling sorry for me. That's not the point.

I'm telling you my story, sharing my act with you, because I want you to become aware that you, also, have an act—we all do. And, realize it or not, your act is running your life!

- Your act is whatever role you've chosen to play in life.
- Your act is the brave front you're using to protect and hide your vulnerability.
- Your act is whoever you've chosen to BE, so you would never be hurt again in the same way.
- Your act is also your ongoing attempt to prove something you thought you needed to prove. But you would have no need to prove that if you could accept that it was already so. It already is!

The trouble with having an act is that it hides the Real You. And the problem with your story is that you made it up at a time in your life when you were not old enough or wise enough to understand the life-altering consequences of your having arrived at such a weighty conclusion.

You'd be wiser than most if you could accept that you do, in fact, have an act, and even wiser still if you realized that your act has you.

How your act came to be

When you were no more than a child, a simple and perhaps insignificant incident triggered a conclusion that was to become the pattern for your life. Something was said or done that hurt your feelings and rattled your cage. As a result of that upsetting experience, you arrived at some inappropriate conclusion about life. That deduction became your set-in-stone reality concept.

Based on that earlier supposition, you decided who you would be and how you would deal with life. But that was merely a child's reactive point of view. Think about that for a moment and allow yourself to see that you are now stuck in the ups and downs of a merry-go-round reality created by a 4-year old.

What if you misinterpreted the significance of that incident and arrived at the wrong conclusion when you were a child?

Then your whole reality concept would be based on a child's tall tale. Think of the consequences if your reality concept is based on an erroneous conclusion. Since that reality concept is what determines the content in your life, you'd be wise to rethink that original conclusion, wouldn't you?

If you're having trouble accepting that you have an act, it's because your act is who you are being. The error is in thinking your act is not an act. Believe me, you have an act. We all do. And your act is a cover-up for the real you.

Your act is the front you present to the world; it's the shield you hide behind to keep from being hurt. In running your act, you'll feel relatively safe as long as you stay hidden behind that false front. In truth, you're hiding because you don't want THEM to find out about your fears, your self-doubts and worries.

The downside of having an act is that no one will ever get to know the real you—but then neither will you.

Trapped in Your Act

So, face it! You DO have an act. We all do. Your act is the role you've chosen to play in the story around which you've built your life. Maybe it's time you thought about how you created your act.

Here's the formula for act creation:

- A childhood incident rattled your cage.
- You came to an erroneous conclusion about life and chose a reality concept.
- You made the BEING decision that created your act.
- You've been replaying that role all your life—trying to prove what?
- The payoff: you get to prove that you're right about life.
- The real results: you keep reaping the same unsatisfactory results over and over and over and over.

The repeating pattern of your life is the price you pay for running your act.

To help you better understand how your act came into being, let's look at how some others created their acts. As you read through these examples, notice there's an incident, the resulting conclusion and then a BEING decision. And then, of course, there are the consequences.

Thach Nguyen's act: "I must prove I am as good as they are."
- **The original incident:** When Thach Nguyen first came to the United States from Vietnam, his parents could not afford nice clothes for him. Some kids in school made fun of his clothes.

- o **His reactive conclusion** and his story: Feeling put down and ashamed, Thach concluded, "I'm not as good as they are."
- o **Thach's knee-jerk decision, the BEING choice**--his act: I will have to prove I'm as good as, or better than they are.
- o **The payoff:** Thach would keep trying to prove he was good enough. In fact, he spent 21 years attempting to prove he was good enough. But that would never be so for him until that moment when he no longer needed to prove it.
- o **The resulting benefit:** Thach achieved financial success far beyond his childhood dreams. So, having that act and proving he was good enough actually made him wealthy.

The finale and the new beginning: Then Thach woke up to what he was trying to prove and decided his act would no longer run his life. Now, Thach no longer needs to prove to himself that he's good enough (his act is no longer needed).

Without the act, his life has taken on a whole different meaning. Although he has always had a powerful desire to make a difference, Thach can now spread his wings and really fly in that way.

You can expect big things from Thach Nguyen as he continues to make a real difference in the world.

But does that mean the good life goes away for Thach, because he's no longer totally focused on the business end of it? Not at all! In fact, the prosperity channel will open even wider for Thach and his manifesting powers will have no limit, because he's not attached to the end results.

Trapped in Your Act

Based on Thach's story, one might assume that all acts are a good thing, but they're not. Some acts are destined to empower you, while others are disempowering. Here's an example of a disempowering act:

Ike Ogut's Act: "proving that women are always unfaithful."

- o **The original incident:** When he was 7, Ike's mother promised to take him to the movies when she got home from work. But while she was at work, he made a mess of the house. When she saw the house in such a state of disorder she became very upset. As punishment, Ike's mom said, *I'm taking your cousin to the movies. You stay home and clean up the house!* Ike was crushed.

- o **Ike's reactive conclusion**—(his story): *If my mother, the one woman I thought I could trust, has betrayed me, then I must assume that no woman is to be trusted!*

- o **Ike's rash decision** (his act): *I'll never trust another woman. Women are unfaithful. They always cheat on their men, so I might as well cheat first.*

- o **The payoff:** Without a clue that he was creating an on-going problem, Ike would spend the next 17 years in and out of failed relationships. Each time, he proved to himself that he was right: *Women are unfaithful creatures that can't be trusted.*

- o **The resulting consequence:** In running his act, Ike denied himself any possibility of having a faithful, loving partner in a lasting relationship. I hope you can see that a long-lasting, loving relationship just could not happen as long as Ike continued on with his act.

The finale and the new beginning: Once Ike remembered the original incident and realized his opinion about women was just a story he made up, he was ready to give up his act for good. He saw how his act was running his life and made a new BEING choice.

I suggested to Ike that the perfect woman for him was out there waiting and immediately available if he could choose to be the one who belonged in that quality relationship. I coached him through the process of visualizing what his perfect mate would be like and who he would be being if he were already attracting that perfect person to him.

He met Esra the very next evening at a party. Does that sound like a fairy tale? It is neither a fairy tale nor a coincidence. That's just the way it works. Once you get clear about what belongs in your life, the Law of Attraction and the Universe will provide it.

Ike and Esra have been in an intimate relationship for over a year now. I'm using the word intimate here in terms of "in-to-me-see." In the last year, Ike and his girl friend have each worked their way through a lot of old stuff, such as jealousy, mistrust and the inability to commit.

They have definitely created the space for each other to be who they each are without any intent to fix or change. The quality space they create for each other is called "unconditional love" and that's the only environment in which real and lasting relationships thrive. Ike and Esra are planning to be married next spring and I'm invited to be their best man.

Ask Ike and he'll tell you that replacing your act with being up front and real is the true path to the good life.

My story and those of Thach and Ike should be enough to convince you that as a kid, you probably made a big deal out of an insignificant incident. You then arrived at some inappropriate conclusion that has become the game plan for the rest of your life. That reactive decision will have become the act that runs your life until you wise up and make a new BEING choice.

Let me give you a few more brief examples. See if one of them fits you!

- o When Ann's mother left Ann with an aunt to go grocery shopping, Ann came to the conclusion that as soon as she dearly loved someone, they would leave her.

  In maintaining that reality concept as a repeating story, Ann would be in one loving relationship after another. Then she would give that person ample reason to leave her without ever realizing or taking responsibility for causing the other person to leave. She set herself up to always be left alone and became the always-abandoned victim of her relationships.

- o Joann's story was that her father beat her. To make that reality concept come true, she married twice. Both husbands beat her. I'm sure I don't have to tell you that she actually set the stage for those beatings so she could play the victim when it happened.

- o Evelyn's story is a little different. She listened to her parents complain that there was never enough. She bought into her parent's victim story and made it her reality concept.

  Evelyn's life then became a repeating pattern of "never having enough." Whenever Evelyn was able to create more income, she'd spend it before it arrived. That way there would not be enough when the extra income showed up and the "never enough" pattern of her life was maintained.

Maybe you've noticed that while some acts make you rich, others actually keep you poor.

Your act can make you rich or poor

The experienced end result will depend on what you're trying to prove. If you were told as a kid that you weren't good enough and you believed that, you'd spend your life proving that you weren't good enough. If that were your act, you'd be doomed to experience life as if you were never quite good enough.

But if you disagreed with that "not good enough" criticism, your BEING decision, (your act) would be, "I'm proving to the world that I AM good enough. With this act, you'd spend your life proving that you were as good as, or even better than THEM.

And, as a result of your act, you'd be living a reality of success and prosperity. But get this: Even though your act made you rich and powerfully successful, that success would not make you happy. That's because no matter how much success you manifested, you'd still be too busy trying to prove that you were good enough, smart enough, or strong enough.

Your act is a trap, because whatever you're trying to prove will never be true for you, until you've become clear that what you were trying to prove never really needed proving. It was already true before you began running your act. You've always been good enough!

On the merry-go-round

Having an act is a little like riding the horse on a merry-go-round. As the horse goes up and down, the merry-go-round goes round and round. The ups and downs are your mood swings. Each revolution is the repeating pattern of the same results you always manifest when running your act. Those results won't change until you step off the merry-go-round

In the meantime, you'll always be reaching out—hoping each time around, you'll catch the brass ring. That brass ring you're reaching for is happiness. But you won't find it because it isn't out there to be found. Chasing happiness is like trying to catch a live blue bird in your hands.

You'll never catch it until you've stopped chasing it. Happiness is not a thing to be found; it's just a BEING choice. Once you've stopped running after it, you'll choose it, and then, the blue bird of happiness will come land on your shoulder.

So far in this discussion, I've been telling you about acts as if you had only one act. Actually, you'll have an act to cover just about any situation. For instance, for my first 6 years in school, my act was that I was dumb.

My I'm dumb act

I don't remember who told me I was dumb, or how I arrived at that conclusion, but I know this: for my first 6 ½ years in school, I stayed busy proving, with bad grades, that school work was hard. I stayed up late studying and got up early in the morning to study again, and I still didn't get it in a way that allowed me to earn the good grades.

I want you to see that my *I'm dumb* act couldn't let school lessons be easy.

To God or As God

Then a seventh grade english teacher asked me to go to the blackboard and diagram a sentence she had been told couldn't be diagrammed. When I surprised her by diagramming it, she acted as though I had created a miracle. She went on and on praising me, telling the whole class how smart I was.

Her praise embarrassed me to the point that I wanted to crawl under my desk and hide. But at some level I accepted her words of praise as the truth, and then a strange thing happened. From that point on, I got A's and B's in school, and I did that without ever having to take a book home.

In the flick of an eyelash, I went from dumb to smart. How can that be? How could a dumb kid suddenly become smart? She didn't put the smarts into me. The fact is, I was never dumb in the first place. But for as long as my "I'm dumb" act was running, I could never have manifested anything but results that would prove I was dumb.

I hope you can see from this example that, for as long as you're running your act, you'll get the same dumb results over and over again.

As individualizations of God, when we arrive at some dumb conclusion about life, we've created our reality. Then, until we change our minds, we are doomed to experience a life filled with whatever belongs with that point of view.

If you could just accept that what you're manifesting (poverty or riches) is merely the effect of your chosen reality concept, then you would see how you could easily change your manifested results to something far better by just changing your mind about what you will believe.

Your reality concept is just a story that you made up along the way. And your act is the protective shell you've built around yourself to survive in that reality.

- o What do you suppose would happen if you simply changed your mind about what's real?
- o What do you suppose would change in your life if you finally accepted that your condition of lack, in any of its forms, is merely the effect of a story you made up as you went along?
- o How powerful would you feel if you gave yourself permission to create a brand-new, happy, prosperous reality in which to experience life?

Happiness is a BEING choice

Did you know that you could choose to be joyful and happy, no matter what the circumstances? You could, but you don't, and you probably won't. Why not? Why aren't you living in that place of bliss right now? Maybe it's because your act is still running your life. And maybe it's because you believe your act is not an act and you can't give it up.

How great would your life be if most of the time you were enthusiastic, joyful and happy? Dwell with that question for a moment, and then ask yourself why you're not already there.

You've been chasing happiness all your life. You'll keep chasing it for as long as you have something you're trying to prove. Enthusiasm, joy and happiness are simply BEING choices. How great would your life be if you were almost always enthusiastic, joyful and happy?

To uncover your act, you might ask yourself what you're trying to prove.

Knowing Your Why

First know why

You wouldn't pack up and move to New York City or San Francisco without a pretty good reason for moving, would you? So, before you attempt to choose out of your current situation into a new reality, you'll want to be clear about what you really want and why you want it.

You should know by now that a change of circumstances for you would require a change in both your reality concept and in your self-concept. To manifest a different set of circumstances, you'll have to change your mindset about who you are and what you believe.

Sounds simple and it is. But if your why is not big and powerful enough, your new BEING choice will never make it past your ego's determined efforts to get you back into the old box. How do you acquire a why that's big enough to motivate you and take you past your ego's powerful resistance to change?

Let's say you were a doctor thinking about retirement, and it quickly dawns on you that you have not saved enough money to retire and maintain your current living standard. That's when you'd realize that to retire and live comfortably, you'd have to create a substantial income from sources other than your practice.

What would need changing before you could begin the process of creating outside sources of income? As a doctor, you would have to stop thinking of yourself as a rich doctor and choose, instead, the identity of a wealthy doctor. And it would be necessary to change your reality concept about how money is earned and how it is spent.

"Trading hours for dollars" is not the ideal earning strategy for becoming wealthy because once you've stopped working, your income stops, too. And if you intend to be wealthy, you'll want to take a look at your spending habits as well. Most people feel rich only when they're spending, so they spend money as fast as they make it.

If you intend to be wealthy, you might want to change your reality concept, relative to your spending habits.

As a doctor, you are probably living high off the hog and rich by most people's standards, but you are not wealthy— meaning you couldn't retire and still live as richly as you do now. And you should know by now that you can never actually be wealthy, until you have chosen to be wealthy.

The benefits of becoming wealthy
To transform your reality concept and your self-image from rich to wealthy, you'll want to get pretty excited about the benefits of being wealthy.

What do wealthy people have that most rich people do not have? If you were thinking "more money", I'm not surprised. That's what almost everyone assumes. But having money to spend is not what makes you wealthy. What makes you wealthy is a constant flow of sufficient residual income to maintain your current living standards without working for it.

So, being wealthy is more about having the time and freedom to enjoy life.

Often, the biggest problem with being rich is that you don't have time to smell the roses. You have very little time for your family or yourself. You keep telling yourself about all the things you'll do when you find the time. But you just never find that time. Let's face it, rich people seldom have enough free time.

My definition of true wealth is
Sufficient passive income to live comfortably,
along with ample time freedom to enjoy your life,
your family and your money.

If you're already rich, what's wrong with that?
Most rich people are trapped in the reality concept of trading hours for dollars. Doctors and lawyers fall into this trap. They seem to have this idea that hard work and money go together like a horse and carriage.

The problem with that point of view is the only way you could have more money would be to work harder and longer. The idea of more hours seems to make sense, until you wake up to the fact that having more money would mean giving up the free time you'd need to enjoy that money—a catch-22 situation.

Knowing Your Why

Most people fall into this reality concept trap and assume there's no way out. There won't be a way out if you keep thinking inside the box of your trading-hours-for-dollars reality concept. It should seem obvious, then, that your transformation from rich to wealthy will require a reality concept change relative to how real money is earned.

Your first and biggest step out of that old box would be for you to accept that being wealthy is simply an out-of-the-box BEING choice. You won't need to know how it will happen, nor will you need to make it happen. But you must come to know that once you've chosen to be wealthy, the Universe will provide the how-to. All you'll have to do is say, "yes", to the opportunities as they show up.

You'd be putting a great deal of faith in the attractor factor. You'd have to know that by simply choosing to BE wealthy, you'd just naturally attract opportunities and circumstances for (easily and naturally) becoming wealthy. It really is that simple. Wealthy is a BEING choice.

Your way out of the trap
Before you can choose to BE wealthy, you must be highly motivated to make that change.

The following is important enough to repeat:
Before you can choose to change your circumstances, you must:
1. Be clear about what you want.
2. Know why you want it.
3. Know beyond the shadow of a doubt that you can have it.
4. And want it so badly you can taste it.

With all four of the above in place, you will just naturally choose into that new reality with a commitment that goes far beyond a simple want.

Once you've made a solid commitment to BE the one enjoying life in that new reality, it is as certain to manifest as night follows day. But stepping into a new reality concept with that level of commitment requires a powerful why.

How do you create your why?
If you are not already rich, create a list of 20 reasons why you want to be rich. If you are already rich, create a list of 20 reasons why you'd want to be wealthy.

When your list is complete, prioritize it and build a vision of how great and wonderful your life would be if you had already manifested the top three items on that list.
- o How would you be enjoying life with your family if you were already wealthy and had ample free time?
- o What are some of the other ways would you be enjoying life more?
- o What kind and quality of clothes would you be wearing?
- o What would you be doing?
- o Where would you go?
- o Where would you live?
- o What would your friends be saying?

You want to be wealthy? Paint a vivid picture of your life as it would be if you were already wealthy and then choose to BE the one in that picture. It doesn't matter whether you're choosing out of poverty into riches or out of rich into wealth, the principle is the same.

Once you've made a solid, committed BEING choice, that new reality must always manifest—if you can find your way past your powerful ego's resistance to that change.

But you must believe, beyond the shadow of a doubt that your new reality choice will manifest. It is for that reason that I suggest that you not take the giant step out of poverty into wealth. Instead, make it a baby step. The next chapter explains the importance of first taking the baby step.

Worth repeating

Most professionals fall into the reality concept trap of trading hours for dollars. They generally have this idea that hard work and money go together like a horse and carriage.

With that belief, the only way you could have more money would be to work harder and longer hours. With this way of thinking about how money is earned, you would just naturally assume there was no way out.

And there won't be until you've changed your reality concept relative to how real money is accumulated.

Your first and biggest step out of that old box would be for you to accept that being wealthy is simply a BEING choice. You need not know how it will happen, and you won't have to make it happen. Just choose to be wealthy, the Universe will provide the how-to and you'll be saying "yes", to those opportunities as they show up.

9. The Baby Step

BEING a god in practice

To truly know God, you must BE a god in all aspects of your life—health, wealth, and relationships. To practice BEING a god, you must take charge of your thoughts moment by moment and learn the art of BEING present, living in the now. Once you've become the observer, you are no longer your ego mind. In your relationships you will learn how to create the space of unconditional love and truly listen.

The power of God in you, passive in nature, is simply the ability to commit to a new way of BEING you. The BEING Principle, combined with the Attraction Principle, makes you awesomely powerful. To discover, unleash, and grow your God power, you must make frequent conscious use of it, on a daily basis, creating and manifesting new realities at will.

Proving it to yourself

To know in theory and believe that you are an individualization of God is an awesome heart-warming revelation. But that belief, in and of itself, won't make a dent in your circumstances—not until you've tested and proven that theory to yourself through demonstrated results.

Your God power, the ability to manifest at will, will grow each time you consciously use that power (the BEING Principle) to make a new BEING choice and to have that new reality manifest, as if by magic. Each time you put your faith in the Attraction Principle and see your new reality made manifest, your confidence and your consciousness will grow.

But it's just another box

To truly know God, you must grow your consciousness, your confidence and your self-worth. The way out of your box, as always, is a BEING choice. But with each new BEING commitment, you've merely created yourself a bigger sandbox in which to play the Game of Life.

The thing to get is that your new reality is just another box, a mere stepping stone on your path to greater confidence, self-worth and a higher consciousness. With each new box created, your tendency will be to settle in and become attached to that new reality. Don't stop there! You're not home yet! You still have more to prove to yourself.

And the material gain you've just manifested is not the real prize. The real win—the victory you'll want to celebrate-is your growth in consciousness, confidence and self-worth. Make up your mind to never get stuck in the status quo again. Instead, immediately after each success, start thinking about your next out-of-the-box adventure.

Are you ready, yet?

At some point in growing your self-worth, your confidence and your consciousness, you'll realize you have nothing left to prove. Until then, just keep creating reasons to celebrate your newly discovered power to BE and your life.

So, back to the present: where are you now? Are you ready to choose out of your box, or have you already chosen out?

If you've truly gotten the message available in this book so far, you should be:

1. Primed and ready to take that quantum leap out of your box.
2. Or maybe you've already taken a leap of faith into a new reality and are now doing battle with your change-resistant ego.
3. Or perhaps you're still trapped in your act, petrified in fear of taking that leap of faith into your dream reality of better health, wealth and more loving relationships.

Whichever the case, for you, I suggest you consider one more thing. Before you make your move, make sure your first move out of that box is something to *really* celebrate.

The baby step
To grow your confidence and your self-worth, we'll need a definitive win. Your first step out of the box should not be a giant leap of faith but, rather, a baby step. The baby step may sound contrary to what I've been telling you about being capable of taking the quantum leap, but think about this:

You've always had awesome manifesting powers and until now, have been almost totally unaware of it. What you've learned about your powers, from reading this book, can only be theory for you until you've proven it to yourself through actual manifested results.

The Baby Step

Your big dreams, in the past, have failed because your powerful change-resistant ego easily arm-wrestled you back into your old box. But this time out of the box, you'll want a win that takes you past that ego resistance. You'll want a win that makes a believer out of you—a win that increases your faith in the process. With total faith in the process you'll be able to choose out of your box again and again.

But before you choose your new reality this time, you must know it can and will manifest. To remind you how powerful you really are, let's review what you've learned so far:

Review:
1. In reading chapter one, you learned that you have the ability to take a quantum leap out of your problem reality into a reality in which your problem of lack no longer exists. If you got that message, you would know that you could solve your problem by simply choosing a new way of BEING you.
2. In chapter two, you may have been inspired with the realization that you are, in fact, an individualization of God with the power to make new BEING choices. You would then know that once you've chosen your new way of BEING you, your new reality must manifest. It's the law!
3. From reading chapter three, you may have been in awe of the fact that your word is actually law in the Universe. You now know all your thoughts and all your spoken words are prayers, and all your prayers are automatically answered.
4. In chapter four, you learned that the will of God is that you discover just how powerful you really are.
5. From chapter five, you learned that the real secret to winning is the winner's attitude, and you learned how to acquire a winner's attitude.

6. From chapter six you learned why the changes you've wanted in the past haven't happened. You have a powerful ego, which you can expect to resist any new attempt to change your mind about who you will be.
7. Then you learned in chapter seven that you have an act; we all do, and your act is now running your life. Your act is a pretense, but it is also your way of proving something you'd have no need to prove if you could allow yourself to see that it's already true.

Trapped by your act

Now you know you have all the power of the Universe behind your "I am" statement, but instead of being free, you've been locked in a cage of your own making. You've previously made your BEING choice, and are now trapped in that reality, a slave to nothing more substantial than your point of view about life.

Most people, (at least 85 percent) will end up back in the old box soon after choosing out because they were not able to make their way past their built-in resistance to change. Or, they'll end up poorer than they wanted to be, staying trapped in the status quo because they haven't found their power of choice and have not, yet, learned their true identity.

But you will be the exception to the rule; you'll beat those odds because you now know the truth. You know you're an individualization of God with the power to take that quantum leap. Unfortunately, you'll still be trapped until you have become a master at dealing with your ego's resistance.

How do you find your way out of your ego's reality concept trap in such a way that will take you past that ego resistance and allow you to stay out? The answer, of course, is to begin with the baby step.

The Baby Step
What you're looking for is certainty
For your first baby step out of that box, you'll choose a goal that's just far enough outside your comfort zone to put you into a sweat. You'll want a goal that stretches you, but not so far out that you'd have any doubt about your ability to manifest your intention, in let's say, the next eight weeks.

The key ingredient to your success is the level of faith you have in your ability to manifest the desired result. As Christ said, *"As thou hast believed, so shall it be done unto thee."*

There is actually no limit to what you can manifest, but there will be a temporary limit to your belief in the process. What you manifest this next time out of the box is not nearly as important as is the degree of certainty you'll want to have about your ability to manifest the intended result.

You will manifest only at the level of your self-confidence, your self-worth, and your certainty in the process. As your certainty grows, so does your consciousness.

Growing more certain
With each result manifested, your belief in the process will grow. As your certainty grows, your self-confidence and your manifesting powers will grow. And with each successful manifestation, you'll find yourself choosing bigger and better goals-all achievable and believable.

You've been making out-of-the-box BEING choices all your life, manifesting the corresponding result, but you've never, until now, given yourself credit for having BEING power. Instead, you've conned yourself into believing each success was merely a product of your DOING activity.

Your ego would have you believe success is all in the doing.

What we're after here is a serious win that will allow you to see that your real power is in your BEING choices—as opposed to your previous idea that it was all about the DOING. You'll be learning to trust the Law of Attraction to do the MAKE-IT-HAPPEN work, once you've made your solid, committed BEING choice.

And then the resistance kicks in

Both before you choose and after you've chosen, your ego's resistance will kick in. To make it past that resistance, you'll be learning new skills. I suggest you do not take your baby step, quite yet, not until you have some clear ideas about how to deal with that resistance.

In the following chapters, you'll be given powerful tools for dealing with ego resistance. For instance:

- o Your ego uses tricks, such as overwhelm and procrastination, to put you into doubt about your ability to accomplish your mission. You'll want to understand ego's tricks so you can deal with them effectively.
- o Your ego will use mind chatter to talk you back into the old box. You'll be learning how to use the Power Pause as your most powerful tool for dealing with that self talk.
- o Your ego uses the emotions of fear, self-doubt and worry in its attempts to scare you back into the old box. You'll find your Powerpact support group is your most effective tool for dealing with ego's fear tactics. Your support group will help to keep you out of the box, fired up and empowered.
- o Your chances of success will improve immeasurably once you've hired yourself a BEING coach who truly

The Baby Step

understands that the path to success is BE DO HAVE, not DO HAVE BE.

You'll find all those tools and more in the following chapters. Before you take your first baby step, I would suggest you read on.

Now it's your turn again
What have your learned so far?

Part II — The Ego Traps

Your ego's resistance to change

Your ego's main job in life is the survival of it's being whoever it perceives itself to be. Its identity is based totally in your current reality concept. Ego perceives its job to be the maintenance or survival of the status quo. Once you've become serious about improving your circumstances, your ego will see that proposed change as a threat to its survival.

Your ego will have two basic survival tactics
1. It will try to prevent your choosing out of your box, (the current reality)
2. and once you've chosen out, your ego will be trying to get you back into your old way of being.

To deal effectively with this ego resistance, you must learn to understand why it resists change and not be surprised when it tries to sabotage your attempt. And once you've wised up to ego's tricks, you'll need a whole arsenal of powerful tools for dealing with its attempts to block your success. You'll find those tools in Part III.

Part II will alert you to ego's many traps, so you can recognize an ego trap once you've fallen into it. You'll find a chapter devoted to each ego trick and you'll learn the tool or tools recommended for dealing with that ego maneuver.

Chapter's 10 through 17--Ego's tricks for keeping you trapped in your current reality—

10 The Pipe Dream Reality

Part II – Ego Traps

Once you've chosen out of the old box with a new BEING commitment, your ego will be using a different tactic. Before you chose, it was trying to convince you there was no way out, but now that you're out, the game will have changed. Your ego will be trying to trick you back into the old box.

At this point, you will have made your commitment to a new way of BEING you, but your ego has not yet bought into your new reality. Ego's new strategy will be clever devices intended to get you back into the old way of being. This tactic works, only when you've fallen into the trap of seeing yourself as your ego.

Ego's traps for getting you back into your box once you've chosen out
   o   Amnesia—you'll forget you have the power to choose
   o   Self-doubt
   o   Mind chatter
   o   Overwhelm
   o   Procrastination
   o   An ego con job—your success is not good enough—
       you couldn't do it again
   o   Forgetting to show up for your Powerpact meetings
   o   Having you forget to use the tools
   o   Hibernating, in a funk, but hiding out—ashamed to
       ask for help

10

The Pipe Dream

REACH FOR THE STARS

The pipe dream goal
…a step too far

The only viable way for you to grow your manifesting powers is by taking one successful progressively larger baby step after another out of your box.

When I first began teaching prosperity workshops years ago, I let participants choose goals that were, for them, unreachable in the short run. That was before I discovered the importance and the necessity of starting with the shorter, but successful baby step rather than one giant leap of faith.

DO YOU have the power to take the quantum leap? Yes, most certainly! But you can only leap as far as your belief will take you in one leap.

Not beyond your ability to believe

For instance the record high for the pole vault remained unbroken for years. For some reason pole-vaulters believed that record would never be beaten. Then one day the record was broken by one man.

As soon as that old mental limit was lifted, several other pole vaulters set new records, which proved you can only jump as high as you can believe.

Years ago, if a workshop participant failed to reach his or her goal, I was naturally disappointed. And of course I wondered why? What went wrong? These principles always work, without fail. If that participant had truly made a new BEING choice, how could he or she fail?

The answer is: Their goal was a pipe dream, and no one ever succeeds beyond his or her ability to believe.

Your ego encourages you to choose a pipe dream

And since your ego wants to keep you confined in your old box, one of its favorite traps is to encourage you to choose a pipe-dream goal—a goal so far outside the box you don't really believe it can or will happen.

As an individualization of God, a fact of life, for you is that, if you don't really believe it will happen, it won't. You will demonstrate only at the level of your own belief.

What's a pipe dream? A pipe dream is the kind of far-out desires a person might dream up while on a high from smoking pot. But you don't have to smoke pot to dream an unreachable goal. Your ego will love your pipe dream!

But don't let this idea of "too big" stop or discourage you from dreaming big! I encourage you to choose big and then take a baby step toward it.

But have you really chosen?

The Universe is set up so that you can and will manifest any reality you can dream up, but only if you truly believe it can and will happen. So, keep dreaming big, but don't choose a short-term goal that's beyond your ability to believe or accept. Your powers are unlimited, however:

- o Your lack of self-confidence will place a limit on your manifesting powers.
- o And your self-limiting self-worth will have set a limit on your ability to accept more good.

Little by little, you'll be raising the limit on your manifesting powers and upping the bar on your self-worth.

One of the tests for determining whether or not you've truly committed is whether or not your ego reacts to that your new BEING choice. If your ego is not threatened by your most recent goal setting, that goal may be a pipe dream. If so, your ego will be very pleased that you've chosen an unreachable goal.

But if your ego is truly upset, it's time to celebrate because your ego's reaction is positive evidence that you've truly chosen out of your box. Now, all you have to do is study up on the rest of your ego's tricks for keeping you boxed into the current reality.

You might want to notice that before your ego can trick you back into your box, it must con you into a state of amnesia. Then you'll be living your life as your ego, once again, because you've forgotten your True Identity.

Worth repeating

Remember: your ego's main intention is to keep you safe from harm. It thinks only in terms of survival. Any new BEING choice is a threat to its survival.

Your ego will have two basic survival tactics
- It will try to prevent your choosing out of your box, (the current reality)
- and once you've chosen out, your ego will be trying to get you back into your old way of being.

In dealing with this ego resistance, you must learn to understand it and not be surprised when it shows up. Once you've wised up to ego's tricks, you'll need some pretty powerful tools for dealing with them.

The intention of Part II is to make you aware of ego's many traps, so you will be able to recognize a trap once you've fallen into it.

11.

You Have Amnesia

It's called amnesia

A great many plots for books and movie scripts are built around a character who has had some sort of a shock, maybe a bump on the head, that caused him to forget who he is. It's called amnesia.

Have you any idea why we are so intrigued by that sort of plot? It's because, at some level of consciousness, we know this is the story of our lives. We all have amnesia. How so? As individualizations of God, we have the power to create new realities at will, but how often do we remember we've got that power?

You've forgotten how powerful you are

We've been creating new realities all our lives, but we keep forgetting how really powerful we are. This is the process:

- o We make a BEING choice that launches a great new reality.
- o We manifest those new circumstances.
- o We revel in our new creation for a while, and then,
- o We once again become attached to whatever reality we've created and forget who we are really.

At some point during this creative process we have been programmed to forget we have the power to change our circumstances with a new BEING choice. Once again we are trapped in a reality of our own making and are taking no responsibility for having created our predicament.

Notice that once you've lost your power of choice, you have amnesia and there will appear to be "no way out."

Why you and I develop amnesia

The Game of Life is set up in a way that encourages our continued growth in consciousness. The process seems to require that we go in and out of consciousness.

For instance: in order to grow your consciousness, you must choose out of your box. Think about that choosing-out step for a moment. You'll see that before you could choose out of your box, you must be IN that box, experiencing life from that point of view.

We must assume we develop amnesia each time out of the box, so we can experience the current reality as though it were real. Then, when ready for a change, we'll have that "aha" moment once again, and rediscover our power of choice. Each trip out of the box brings us to a new level of conscious awareness.

With each out-of-the-box venture, we'll grow a little more aware of our true identity. But, with each time out, we've merely created a bigger box in which to play at the Game of Life. We create our new box, live in it for a while, become attached and remain stuck until we've found the courage to detach and move on. What's the point of all this?

Imagine climbing a grand set of stairs that, with each step up, allowed you to gain a whole new perspective on life. And from that new level of self-awareness you'd just have to spend some time enjoying life in that exciting new reality with your brand-new view of life.

The creative process

Growing your consciousness is never a giant leap to the top of the stairs. It is just a process of your taking the next step, choosing out of your box whenever you're ready to detach from the status quo and move on.

That "aha" moment—your growth in consciousness—will happen in that instant when you've, once again, awakened to the realization that you have the power to choose to be YOU in a brand new way—in an exciting new reality.

The creative process for mankind is BE DO HAVE. This is the only order of creation that works for us, and each step in the creative process is essential to the next step. You can't skip any of the steps. You must BE before you can DO and DO before you can HAVE.

Where we get stuck

It is in the HAVING part of the cycle that we become attached, and then we're stuck, unwilling to let go of our attachment to the status quo. Detaching is essential to the creative process and it is the most difficult step. Notice that you cannot get to where you want to be without leaving where you are now.

To grow your consciousness, you must move beyond the HAVING and into a new way of BEING YOU. To create the space for being YOU in a brand-new way, you must be able to destroy your attachment to whomever and whatever you have become attached.

This does not mean you must destroy a relationship in order to detach. Nor does it mean you must give up all possessions before choosing something new. It does mean you must detach from needing him, her or it, so you can, then, experience a life in a different context. Once detached, you will still have it all, but are no longer coming from need.

If you want life to get better in some way, detach from your current identity so you can be you in a brand-new way.

Create persist destroy

To help you understand why we develop amnesia from time to time, let's look at the BE DO HAVE creative process as a series of out-of-your-box adventures.

BE DO HAVE, as a repeating cycle, is now CREATE PERSIST DESTROY. In comparing the two, BE becomes CREATE; DO becomes PERSIST; and HAVE becomes DESTROY. (Once you have it; IT has you)

The cycle can begin again just as soon as you are able to detach. Once you've learned to HAVE and not be attached to the HAVING, you will be a free soul. And once again, you'll be free to move on to your next daring adventure.

I hope you can see that once you're hooked, locked into the status quo, the HAVING has you. Once again, you will have developed amnesia and your ego is back in charge. Ego will then play its trump card called, "You are now stuck in the status quo, and there's no way out."

12.

Your Reality Concept

Boxed In

Has You Boxed In

There's no way out

Your ego's greatest con job, made possible only because you have amnesia, is: *"There's just no way out of my current situation!"* How many times in your life have you been stuck in the status quo because you believed there was no way out of those circumstances?

How about now? Are you stuck in a relationship, a job, or financial circumstances that apparently have no solution? You might want to notice how ridiculous your predicament is, considering the fact that you are an individualization of God with the power to make a new BEING choice that would solve your problem.

The amazing thing about believing there's no way out is that you've been choosing your way out of undesirable circumstances, making out-of-the-box BEING decisions all your life. And each time out of that old box you've manifested a brand-new reality and a new set of circumstances.

The trap

You had the power and now you've lost it! You've forgotten how to choose! Seems a silly trap to be in, doesn't it?

It's the same old story. Once settled in that new box, you were trapped again. You've forgotten you solved your last big problem with a new BEING commitment. Well, you've found your power of choice before and you can do it again.

The way out of "no way out" is to remember who you are. Really! You have the power—you've always had it—but you keep forgetting you have it. Maybe now, this very moment, it's time you remembered once again, who you are!

But now you know

Now, you are wise enough to know you were programmed to forget, so you could gradually grow in consciousness, taking baby steps until you've grown wise enough to use the power wisely and lovingly. Now it's time to remember that your ego needs you powerless so it can maintain the illusion of your latest reality manifestation.

Your reality and mine are mere illusions maintained by an ego good at its job. After all, poverty in any of its forms could not be your reality if that illusion did not seem real to you.

The way out is to remember that you are an individualization of God with awesome powers. Once there in consciousness, the illusion of lack in any of its forms will be a joke.

You keep forgetting who you really are, so you can truly experience your latest reality creation as real. You forget so you can be reborn with a new awakening. And you won't be finding your way out of that box until you remember, once again, that you really do have the power to create and manifest any reality you can dream up.

If you are fed up with your current circumstances, just remember who you are and choose again!

Remember, "No way out" is just one of ego's many tricks for keeping you in that old box. Chapter 13 will help you understand your, "But I don't know how" ego success barrier.

Ego's Traps

Ego's tricks to keep you in the box

The pipe dream goal
You have amnesia
There's no way out
I don't know how
Mind chatter
Overwhelm
Procrastination
The ego con job (Those results are not good enough)

<u>Now it's your turn</u>

What's your greatest 'ah ha' so far?

But I don't know how!

You say you don't know how?

One of ego's favorite stories is, *I can't choose to be wealthy because I don't know how! I can't BE wealthy, because I don't know how to make it happen!*

But, I don't know how is a story your ego made up to keep you from choosing out of your box. You've been making BEING choices all your life, such as when you chose to be someone who could ride a bike or ski or swim. You didn't know how to do any of those things before you chose, did you?

If you decided to visit your sister in San Francisco, you'd first make up your mind to go, and then you'd work on the "how to," wouldn't you? That's the way life works: first the BEING commitment, and then you'll deal with the "how to" as you travel the path toward your goal.

Don't Know How?

It's just not your job to know the "how to" before you make BEING decisions. Your job, as an individualization of God, is to make the BEING commitment; the Universe will then reveal the "how to" as you go along. Then you'll just be taking whatever inspired action shows up for doing the "how to" part.

So if your desire is to be wealthy, just choose to be wealthy. Do it, now. The "how to" will show up in the form of opportunities, and they'll come to you automatically without effort. You'll be enthusiastically responding to those prospects as they show up with *"Yes, yes, and yes."*

Your greatest barrier to having life be this simple is your attachment to the idea that you have to make it happen. If the truth were known, you probably have your whole identity tied into *"if it's going to be, it's up to me."* Being a "make it happen" guy or gal is what makes you feel important. That's just who you are and that IS a hard nut to crack, believe me!

Been there; done that

For 29 years, I was owner/manager of a tile business with over 100 employees in Albuquerque, NM. Before I woke up to the secret of the BEING choice and just letting it happen, I worked 12 to 14 hours a day for 15 years at making it happen. My "make it happen" ego identity took a big blow when net profits tripled after I semi-retired, reducing my working hours from 14 to just 4 hours a day.

To get yourself past your "make it happen" success barrier, you must give up your "if it is to be, it's up to me" identity in favor of a new "let it happen" BEING choice—one that would allow the Universe to provide.

Learn to just make your new BEING choice. Once you've allowed yourself to see that's how it works, you will have found the easy way to manifest success. And, believe me! Life really is that simple!

Just choose the results you want. Make your new BEING commitment, and then turn the delivery process over to the Universe. Success is not the, "grit your teeth, nose to the grindstone, get it done, or else" process your ego would have you believe.

Your ego thinks money and hard work are related, but your ego has it wrong. Great successes are never about you making it happen. They're about you making the truly committed BEING choice and then letting it happen.

Your ego doesn't want you to know life is that simple! To amp up your manifesting powers, you must focus on increasing three things;

1. Your faith in principle (The BEING Principle, and The Attraction Principle).
2. Growing your self-confidence to the point of allowing you to choose to BE wealthy.
3. Growing your self-worth to the point that would allow you to accept the path to wealth when it shows up in your life.

No limit to the supply
Your current inability to choose an out-of-the-box goal is not a measure of what the Universe can deliver, it's a measure of what your self-worth will allow you to accept. For the Universe, there is no limit to the supply. The only limit in place is the one you've placed on what you can allow yourself to choose and accept.

Don't Know How?

The only real way to grow your self-worth and increase your faith in the process is by proving your manifesting powers with baby steps that become your manifested reality. Your self-confidence, your faith and your self-worth will grow with each successful manifestation.

Before moving on to the next chapter, be sure you're clear that your further success in any of its forms would require a new BEING commitment. To change from a "make it happen" person to a "let go and let the Universe deliver" way of being would require a transformation in consciousness—a new BEING choice—a new way of being you.

You'd have to give up your identity as a "make it happen" mover and shaker in favor of the passive, choose and let the Universe provide, way of being. Can you make that BEING choice now into the stress-less life? If you intend to make that commitment, now would be a good time.

In the next chapter you'll learn how your ego uses mind chatter to talk you back into the old box.

14.

Mind chatter is
- o Self-talk.
- o That little voice in the back of your head that's telling you why you couldn't, wouldn't or shouldn't do what you've chosen to do.
- o Mind chatter is ego second-guessing your out-of-the-box decisions.
- o Your ego trying to talk you back into the old box.

In addition to fear, worry and self-doubt, your ego will be using mind chatter either to keep you in the old box or to talk you back into it. Self-talk is not an occasional thing. It goes on constantly whether we are aware of it or not.

Once you've begun paying attention to the mind chatter, you'll realize why you're still stuck in the status-quo. Those thoughts are what keep you boxed in. To live your life in a more desirable reality would require a different way of thinking. Your ego will be using mind chatter to second guess any decision to change the way you think.

Realize it or not, your ultimate purpose in life is to take control of your thinking.

Once you start listening to your thoughts, you'll notice a definite pattern to them. Those thoughts set the pattern for your experience. As individualizations of God, we become what we think about; the pattern of your thoughts is who you are being and/or in the process of becoming.

A change of circumstances requires, first, a new BEING commitment—a new way of being YOU in the reality of far better circumstances. That self-concept change is in fact, a change in the pattern of your thinking.

Your first step out of the old way of being you is a new BEING choice, and your second step is to begin listening to what your ego thinks about that change. At this stage in your evolving, you'll want to remember that it is your spirit that chooses out of the box, and it is your ego that will by trying to get you back into the old reality.

The tool
In another chapter, you'll find the Power Pause, the perfect tool for changing the pattern of your thoughts. With the Power Pause, you'll easily step out of your ego's mind-chatter trap, you'll visualize a far better reality, and then you'll choose to BE the one in that new reality.

Once you've mastered the Power Pause habit, you'll change your moods—almost instantly—out of self-doubt and into to self-confidence. And if you're paying attention, you'll notice that your newly found self-confidence is manifesting almost immediate results.

15. Overwhelmed?

Overwhelmed by too much to do?

One of your ego's favorite tactics for tricking you back into the old box is to put you into overwhelm every time your "to do" list gets bigger. When inundated with things that must be done now (or so it seems), your ego will use this opportunity to make your situation seem hopeless.

Your ego will look for every opportunity to discourage your most recent out-of-the-box venture. And your ego will see your expanded "to do" list as an excellent opportunity to play its trump card called "overwhelm."

A defeatist attitude

But overwhelm is nothing more than a defeatist attitude that begins with the fear that you won't get it all done. Being snowed under is just a story your ego will use every time you get a little too much to do stuff on your plate. How do you deal with this ego fear tactic?

Overwhelmed?

No one ever gets it all done, or even expects to. Your response to this ego ploy should be,

So I won't get to all of it today; so what!
What I don't get done today can wait till tomorrow.

Maybe the following story will help you see your overwhelm in a different light.

A consulting job

After running my own successful business for 15 years, I promoted my office manager to general manager and semi-retired, choosing to work only four hours a day instead of 14. And since I then had the free time, I occasionally offered my services as a management consultant.

A chiropractor friend who wanted to increase his business by 25 percent became one of those consulting jobs. I was his prosperity coach, and he now wanted my help in making that transition. I agreed if he would raise his sights to that of doubling his business.

We set the goal

The idea of that much of an increase rattled his belief system big time until I pointed out that he was already handling twice the usual patients on his partner's day off.

For our first step, I scheduled a meeting with him and his two employees to announce the new goal. As expected, both his receptionist and his bookkeeper were totally stressed out and put into overwhelm by the idea of doubling the business.

Overwhelm

His receptionist/office manager quit on the spot, probably because she hadn't been consulted prior to his making that doubling decision. And his bookkeeper broke into tears, saying, *I love my job, but there's no way I can handle twice the work load!*

It became my job to convince her otherwise. In two hours of coaching I convinced her that the current way of handling the patient paperwork was totally inefficient. I suggested a new piece of equipment that would cut her per-patient insurance paperwork in half.

The benefits

I guessed she'd have more job satisfaction, and suggested that perhaps the increased income from doubling the business would result in a healthy salary increase for her. Finally, doubling the business made sense to her. She finally bought into the idea and even became enthusiastic about having a new job experience.

We hired a new receptionist, and by the end of the third month, my friend, the chiropractor, was doing twice the business. A side benefit of this business expansion was the powerful transformation in consciousness of both the chiropractor and his bookkeeper.

Not without a transformation

You must see that there was no way she could have done the new job without a transformation in consciousness. And that's what happened. She totally changed her mind about herself, and a once very shy, milquetoast, no-personality bookkeeper blossomed into an exciting, self-confident woman.

In those two hours of overwhelm and tears, her ego died, and she was reborn into a new way of being. In that moment of transition from "no-way-I-can-do-it" to "yes I can!", she blossomed into a truly alive, vibrant female with the charming personality to match.

Two transformations
In a period of three months she went from no boyfriends to many, from a "nobody" to a very popular young lady. Her transformation was my pay for helping my friend double his business.

The chiropractor moved into a much nicer facility, and continued to expand his business. His partner stayed in the old building and they both became very successful.

How about you?
If this example has you thinking about doubling your sales, the process begins with a BEING choice. As I said in a previous chapter, you do not need to know how it can happen. You only need to believe it can and will happen. Then from that level of certainty, you'll find the courage to make your BEING commitment.

The change you want can only happen as a result of your transformation in consciousness. In choosing to double your sales, you will have changed your mind about who you are, big time.

Renegotiating with your staff
But the idea of doubling your business will just naturally put your staff into overwhelm. When you announce that intention, be ready to renegotiate with your staff and employees or lose them. Even then, some employees may not be willing to go along with the change. You'll be replacing them. That's just part of the growing process. You'll have to make that okay with yourself.

Those who stay will need a new job description. Discern how the increase in business volume will affect them and their job. Suggest a way for them to easily handle the increased business and support you in that growing. You'll want them to share in the benefits and desire the increase as much as you do.

If they're keepers, they'll grow in consciousness with you, and will have some excellent suggestions on how to handle the increase. Before you announce your intentions, you'll want to figure out how your staff and employees will benefit from the increase in business—how perhaps they'll share in the increased profits—and let them know that up front.

If you don't have a staff, you may want to consider hiring a key person to manage your business while you maintain the vision that keeps your business alive and growing.

But I have to do it all myself
Overwhelm comes from thinking, "I have to do it all myself and that there will be some sort of severe penalty or consequence if I don't get it all done". Of course, those imagined penalties are not real. They're just a story your ego made up to get you back in the old box.

The logic for dealing with overwhelm is that almost everybody has more to do than they'll ever get done. Nobody gets it all done! The attitude you'll want to assume for dealing with overwhelm is "So what if I don't get it all done? No big deal!"

Ego in charge
Notice when you are into the panic of overwhelm, your ego is definitely in charge. Step back out of that ego trap and be the observer. You'll want to think of your ego as your six-

year-old inner child who is very much afraid of the terrible consequences if it doesn't get all of it done—and then smile.

When you make your to-do list, prioritize that list. Make it totally okay that you don't get it all done today. Then begin by doing the most important things first.

The easy button

The interesting thing about making it okay that you don't get it all done is that you'll probably get all that done and more, simply because you've taken stress out of the equation. You've just punched your own easy button.

In fact, with fear out of the way, you'll be utterly amazed at how much actually gets done, and notice that some of it gets done without you doing it.

To stay out of overwhelm, you might want to go to Staples and buy yourself an easy button.

If you've set a goal and have been procrastinating on the doing part, Chapter 16 will help you understand why.

16. Procrastination

Ego   You

Procrastination could mean you lack commitment

If you are procrastinating, your ego is sabotaging your out-of-the-box intentions. But more often than not, when you are dragging your feet on the DOING, it is a pretty clear indication that you're not really all that committed to the end result you say you want.

Your ego's delaying tactics may indicate you've got the creative process backwards. Maybe you're attempting a DO HAVE BE creation, which never really works. The creative process, for mankind, as always is BE DO HAVE.

If what you've chosen to do to further your success seems like a chore, you've probably not made a solid BEING commitment. For instance, if you've decided to go on a diet intending to lose 15 pounds, without the appropriate and prior BEING commitment, you'll probably fizzle out on that intention before the job is done.

Or, if you actually succeed in accomplishing your weight loss out of sheer will power, without first having made the appropriate BEING commitment, you can bet the pounds will come right back on with a vengeance. If you've ever gone on a diet, succeeded, and later noticed that you now weigh even more than before the diet, you'll know what I mean.

Try reactivating your vision

If you are sincere about wanting to lose 15 pounds, start by creating an image of yourself weighing 15 pounds less. Picture what new clothes you would be wearing. An example might be to buy a size-smaller bikini swim-suit and thumb tack it to the wall as a reminder

To make the vision more real, see if you can imagine hearing your friends and associates compliment you on the way you look. Picture how much more energy you'd have at that lower weight. Allow yourself to feel 15 pounds lighter and then choose to BE that slimmer person.

Now, having made your BEING commitment, the pounds will come off easily without effort because they no longer belong with your new identity.

Procrastination is often an indication that you have not yet chosen to BE the one who will HAVE that benefit. If you had truly chosen to BE the one who succeeds at the next level, you'd jump out of bed in the morning with that "Can't wait to get at it," attitude. You'd be excited about what was next on your to DO list and couldn't wait to get at it.

If you are procrastinating the DOING, you might want to reexamine your BEING commitment. Perhaps you've only chosen to BE someone who "wants."

Your ego may be running a con. Find out how in Chapter 17.

17. Ego's Con Job

maybe it was just a fluke

Is your ego running a con?

If at this point in your reading of this book, you've already chosen out of your box, your ego will have had to change its tactics. It can no longer stop you from choosing out of the box, because you're already out. Now you can expect your ego to try to con you back into the old box.

Once you've truly made a committed BEING choice, your new reality must manifest. It's the law! So, if you've actually chosen, you can expect one of the following three things to show up in your life:

1. You will have seen positive evidence of your new BEING choice, a manifestation of sorts.
2. Your ego will be reacting and upset, kicking up a fuss in its attempt to get you back into the old box.
3. Or you will have seen the positive evidence, but your ego will still be giving you a hard time, telling you it's not good enough.

Your ego will know you've had a manifestation and that you should be celebrating, but in its last ditch effort to get you back in the old box, your ego will do its best to convince you that nothing has really changed—your being commitment really didn't work. (That's your ego attempting to con you back into the old box.)

In other words, if everything is normal for you at this point in the game (at this stage in your transformation process) your ego will be running a con.

Mr. "Yeah, But"

For instance, your ego might acknowledge your success and then say,

> *Yeah, you've had some success, but your goal was to get to New York, and you didn't really get all the way there!*
> *Yeah, you got tomatoes, but they are not ripe.*
> *Yeah, you reached your goal, but it was just a fluke. You couldn't do it again.*

An appropriate name for your ego at this time might be **Mr. "Yeah, But."** What's your ego telling you? If you have a support group, you might want to share your ego's attempted con with them. If their egos are running cons, they may be different cons than yours.

You'll want to compare ego cons and make a list. By making a list, each of your support group will see some other ways egos might be hoping to sabotage your most recent success.

What is your ego's con?

If you've truly made a BEING commitment and have something to celebrate, your ego will be belittling your

success. It wants to convince you that your win was insignificant and maybe even a fluke.

It is important that you be able to step back and observe ego's antics at this stage of the game. Your attitude about your win will improve significantly if you can smile at your ego's attempted con.

In the next part of this book you'll be given all the tools for dealing with each of ego's games. One of those powerful tools is a support group called a Powerpact. You'll want to share your ego's con with your Powerpact partners. When you do, you might want to ask them what tool they've used to deal with their ego's con.

The tools you might want to use against the con

- Your Powerpact partners will help you see the con if you haven't seen it yet, and they'll give you powerful moral support in dealing with your ego's con game.
- Being an objective observer will allow you to see the attempted con as ego's problem, and you now know, you are not your ego
- A quick way to silence the mind chatter is to ask your ego, *Is that really so?*
- You'll find the Power Pause to be a powerful tool for replacing the fear or self-doubt that may show up as a result of ego's con job.

You might want to ask your support group which of those tools worked best for them. Their success with that tool may encourage you to start using it.

And now, the tools… .

Part III — Dealing With Ego
...The Tools

Tools for staying out of ego's traps

My friend, the devil
The name of my first book, *'So, Why Aren't You Rich?*—before I chickened out on that title—was, *'My Friend The Devil'*. I don't know if you've realized it or not, but Christ was talking to his ego when he said *Get thee behind me satin.*

One tools for taking charge of your life is to acquire the habit of talking to your ego. Notice, you can't be your ego and talk to your ego at the same time. With that tool, in that moment of being objective, you've just put the Real You in charge.

If you're average, your ego will be in charge of your thoughts at least 98% of the time, and spirit, maybe 2%, if that much. To take charge of your life, you'll want to substantially change those odds. You'll want to put your True Self in charge, and then begin the process of retraining your ego.

Is your ego jerking you around?

I like to think training your ego is a little like training your dog. So, whenever your dog decides to take charge of the walk, just gently jerk on the leash and your dog will get the message—you are taking charge of the walk. This tactic works with your ego, as well.

You may want to begin by taking a, who's-in-charge inventory. Here are some questions you might want to consider asking yourself the following questions:

- o *What percent of the time is my ego in charge of my life?*
- o *Has that percentage improved recently?*
- o *Am I willing to let my ego keep jerking me around?*
- o *Or am I ready to take charge?*

If you're ready to take charge and become the Master of Your Life, you might want to take on the following three intentions:

1. To grow your consciousness by demonstrating your manifesting powers, daily, and with each manifested result, to become more and more consciously aware of your True Identity
2. To take back the controls--every day increasing the percentage of time the Real You, not your ego, is in charge of your life
3. To become a master in dealing with your ego's manipulative tricks for getting you back into the box

Ego's Con Job

Make up your mind that your ego will be your servant, not your master. In taking charge, you'll become the master of your life. The following are the tools you'll be given in Part III, for dealing with your ego's antics.

Your tools for dealing with ego
18. Uncovering Your Act
19. You Are Not Your ego
20. Name Your Ego
21. The Power Pause
22. The Powerpact
23. Your Money Barriers
24. You'll Need A Coach

Your most powerful tools for dealing with your ego's resistance to change are:
1. Your Powerpact support group
2. The Power Pause

Changing who you are being will require a change in the pattern of your thinking. Until now, your ego has been in charge of your thinking 24/7. Your job will be to gradually change the pattern of your thoughts increasing the frequency of having the Real You in charge of your thinking.

Suggestions for moment to moment dealing with ego antics
o Choose to live in the now
o Give your ego a name
o Talk to your ego
o Talk to your Powerpact partners

Of course, your transformation begins in that moment when you make up your mind to take over the controls.

One of ego's on-going traps is your story—your act

As a small child, you reacted to life in a way, that decided who you would be from then on, or until you changed your mind. You came to an erroneous conclusion about life and how you would have to deal with it in order to survive. Maybe now you're ready to rethink that four-year-old's conclusion!

Your ego made the decision long ago that to endure and prevail, you would have to prove that you were good enough, smart enough, or loveable enough. Your act—your on-going need to prove yourself in some way-has become your reality trap, a self perpetuating pattern for your life.

And because your self-concept and your reality concept determine what you may have in your life, you are destined to keep on manifesting the same need-to-prove reality—until you decide to uncover and discontinue running your act.

The tool

In order to figure out what your act is, you might want to ask yourself:

- *What am I trying to prove?*
    o *That I'm good enough?*
    o *Or that I'm not?*

Then ask yourself:
- *What's the payoff? (What am I proving to myself?)*
    o *That life is wonderful?*
    o *Or that it isn't?*
(In either case, you get to be right!)

Then, ask yourself:
- *Do I really want to continue running that act?*
- *Or do I want to be real and see where that takes me?*

Here are some problems that come with having an act:
    o Keeping up a pretense is a powerful energy drain.
    o Pretending is disempowering because you're not being real.
    o The people you love and care about won't ever know the real you.
    o You won't ever know the real you.
    o Not knowing the real you defeats the self-discovery process, the true purpose of The Game of Life.
    o Others, who are being real, will see through your act and label you a phony.

To help you see through your own act, here are more examples of fairly common acts people run:
    o I'll feel rich only when I'm spending the money.
    o I'm worthless or I'm not.
    o I'm unlovable or I'm loveable.
    o I'm not good enough or I'm better than.
    o I'm a klutz or I'm not.
    o I'm too short, or too tall.

- o I'm dumb or I'm smart.
- o If I never set a goal, I'll never be disappointed.
- o There will never, ever be enough.

The irony of your act is that you're already good enough, smart enough, and loveable enough, <u>but that can never be so for you until you've given up your need to prove it.</u>

Think about that for a minute! How great would life be for you if you had nothing left to prove? What if your manifesting powers were proven beyond the shadow of a doubt, and you were so certain about life that you could spend the rest of your life helping others find that level of certainty? I mean, you'd really be making a difference!

Your enthusiasm joy and happiness is God expressing Himself in and through you as you. And life just can't get any better than that!

Now it's your turn again

What have your learned so far?

19. You are Not Ego

YOU   YOUR EGO

Remind yourself

The best and most effective way for dealing with ego's persistent efforts to get you back into the old box: is each time ego resistance shows up—whether in the form of, fear, self-doubt, worry or mind chatter—**remind yourself that you are not your ego.**

Instead, know that you are an individualization of a God who experiences life in and through you as you. Ego is your servant, not your master. Each time the resistance shows up, you'll want to remind yourself of the truth of your being and put the Real You back in charge of the moment.

When your ego has you running scared or in self-doubt, that's your signal to remember that you are not your ego. Anytime you're feeling afraid, worried or in a state of overwhelm, that's your ego's problem, not yours.

Ego's tricks work only if you fall into the trap of being your ego—only if you forget to remember that you are not your ego. Remind yourself that the way out of ego's trap is to be objective. Each time you step back and take charge of your thoughts, as the observer, the Real You is in charge.

And now that you're back in charge, congratulate yourself!

A reason to celebrate
Believe it or not, ego resistance is something to celebrate. Why?

Ego resistance is a clear indication that you've actually chosen out of your box with a new BEING commitment.

The rule for taking charge is clear:
> **When fear or self-doubt rears its ugly head, remember you are not your ego and be objective. Getting real in that moment puts you back in charge!**

Ego
Your six-year-old inner child

20. Name Your Ego

Give your ego a name
and then sell it on your new game

Naming your ego

In the last chapter, you learned the steps for taking over the controls from your ego—first, be an objective observer—and remind yourself that you are not your ego. Then, with taking charge in mind, you'll want to listen to that mind chatter, paying close attention to your reactive emotions, such as anger, fear, self-doubt and worry.

As the one in charge of the moment, you'll want to begin talking to your ego, reassuring it, selling it on the benefits of how great life will be when you are finally living in the reality of your latest goal in life. Once your ego accepts your latest intentions as the reality to defend, it will prove to be your best friend by providing you with that experience.

Name Your Ego

But until your ego buys into your new goal, it will fear the change you want and resist with all its considerable clout.

The real problem with ego resistance is that it will seem to be you that's doing the resisting. The resistance will seem to be you at cross-purposes to the change you want.

That's because you've been living your life as your ego. And you've spent most your life looking at life's situations from ego's point of view. Now, you, being your ego is a deeply ingrained habit—a habit you'll want to break.

Up until now, when ego expressed self-doubt, you hadn't realized that you were not the one doing the doubting. Ego's fears were your fears. You experienced being emotionally upset because you were being your ego. You saw reality only through ego's eyes.

But you are not your ego. The Real You is the spirit of God in you. But being a god is not your natural habit, at least, not yet.

You'll want to gradually take over the controls, making it your intention to increase the frequency of times when the Real You IS in charge. In taking charge, you'll want to keep reminding yourself of the truth of your being, and you'll want to keep doing that, until it becomes your new habitual way of being YOU.

Old habits not easy to break
Don't expect to be taking full charge from this moment on. Old habits are not that easy to break. Just make it your intention to take charge of the moment from time to time. With that intention in mind, the frequency and the length of those moments will gradually increase.

To God or As God

But know this: the process of taking over can only begin after you've made it your intention to put the Real You in charge.

Taking control begins with you paying attention as the observer. Whenever ego expresses anger, self-doubt, fear or worry you'll want to step back, and as the observer, realize that you are not the one who's angry or afraid.

And as the objective observer, you'll be convincing your ego that there really is nothing to fear or be angry about. You'll be showing your ego friend that there is no boogie man in the closet, nothing hiding under the bed.

And now, since you'll be talking often to your ego, you will want to give your friend a name. What kind of name would you give a friend who is always there wanting only to keep you safe from harm?

Think of your ego as your six-year-old inner child and give it a name that reminds you of your fearful self when you were six years old. If you had a nickname you might want to use that name for your ego.

For the time being, your ego is your opponent because you've stepped out of the box. You've changed your mind about who you will BE.

Ego's job is to keep you in the status quo, safe from harm. And your most recent goal threatens the status quo. Your ego will be upset and afraid as a result of those intentions. You can expect it to resist the change you want until you've finally sold it on accepting the change as its new reality.

If you want your ego to change, do not argue or fight it. Instead, understand its resistance to the change you want as you would lovingly understand the fears of your six-year-old child. Sell your ego on the change you want; don't just tell it. Reassure it. Take away its fears. Treat it like you would a friend you're wanting to encourage.

Treat your ego as your six-year-old inner child, but while you're being gentle, remember that your ego is also powerful in its ability to resist the change you want.

Later in this book, you'll find a chapter on unconditional love, which is the space created for another to be who he or she is with no intent to fix or change him or her. Strange as it may seem, the space of unconditional love is the only true catalyst for change.

So, if you want your ego to change, the first step in the process would be to make it okay that it doesn't change. That approach won't seem logical until you realize that your ego is powerful in its ability to resist.

So you, resisting that resistance won't solve your problem.

When you remove your resistance to ego's tactics by applying unconditional love to your ego, it will have nothing to resist, and in that space of non resistance you can expect it to listen to reason.

So now that you've learned how to be your ego's best friend, what name will YOU give your friend? Do not put this off. Naming your ego is a very important step in the process of taking charge. So, do it now, or you may forget.

In case you've forgotten why you're naming your ego; remember you cannot be talking to your ego and be your ego at the same time.

21. The Power Pause

A magic wand?

If I offered you a simple, easy-to-use tool that would allow you to transform the outcome of the next moment, what would that be worth to you?

If you could transform the quality of your life moment by moment, how powerful would you be, and what would your life look like if you had the power to change it? The Power Pause is that transformational tool!

Before I tell you about the Power Pause and why its magic works, I want you to imagine your life as a salesperson who had a simple, easy to use magic tool for doubling your sales.

And if you think you're not a salesperson, think again. Every moment of every day, you are selling yourself—if not to someone else, then to yourself. Did you know that part of your job in life is to sell you to you? You didn't?

In what way would your life improve if you had more confidence?

The Power Pause is the perfect tool for growing your confidence *and* improving your sales! But what if I told you your use of the Power Pause would allow you to pre-determine and then manifest the desired outcome for each and every sales call. Would I have your attention?

If you had the power to change the outcome of each phone call even after the phone rang, and before you picked up the phone, would you feel like you had a magic wand? Believe me, the Power Pause is that magic wand!

Power Pause BEING solution examples
In one of our BEING workshop calls, I suggested that insurance salesman Ron Jeffrey use the Power Pause to visualize positive results prior to making each sales call.

One week later, Ron reported back to the class that his use of the Power Pause prior to each sales call had tripled his sales for that week.

In another example, I suggested to a frustrated tennis player that she might want to use the Power Pause to visualize the outcome prior to returning each of her Coach's serves. Net result: (no pun intended) she beat her coach in their very next match, something she'd never done before.

Her coach was amazed and in awe of her student's newly discovered skills, but not surprised when she learned how she'd been beaten. The Power Pause is truly a magic wand for transforming the quality of your life moment by moment.

In yet another example, an author friend, who had needed a cane for a year to walk, used the Power Pause. Three days later, he threw away his cane.

To God or As God

I wouldn't be surprised if you could use the Power Pause as a cure for cancer. I'm not kidding! Two of my friends actually amazed their doctors by curing themselves of cancer.

What is a Power Pause?
...and why is it a powerful transformational tool?
The Power Pause is an easy to use, three-step process for changing the pattern of your thinking. Why is that important?

When you change how you think, you change who you are being, and that simple BEING shift changes your concept of reality. Your new reality concept sends a new message to the Universe, and it then automatically delivers new content that would naturally belong with that reality concept.

If you have any desire to change your circumstances, the Power Pause is your perfect tool for the job!

Why is the Power Pause so powerful?
As individualizations of God, we just naturally become what we think about. And once we've changed our mind about who we will be, a Universe that doesn't know how to say "NO," delivers the appropriate content for that reality context.

The Power of God in you is called the BEING Principle; that's the power you have to choose who you will be. By now, you may have realized just how powerful that makes you.

You have the power in any moment of *now* to change your mind about who you will be, and then to know without a doubt that your reality concept will manifest as a material reality. You truly have the power to change the quality of your next moment, the quality of your day and the quality of your life.

The Power Pause

Well, if you are truly that powerful, why haven't you already done that?

Why haven't you already changed?

The problem is, you've already chosen, and now a powerful part of you does not want you changing your mind about who you will be. Your ego will be as determined to prevent the change you want as you are to have it.

If you truly intend to manifest your desires, you must be able to overcome your ego's powerful resistance to that intended change. In fact, if you are to experience living your life in that new reality, you must be able to sell your ego on that BEING switch.

If you're thinking you are not a salesperson, think again. If you want the quality of your life to change, you must be able to sell your ego past its fears and into accepting that life will be greater and much more enjoyable in that new reality.

But ego is a hard sell

Your ego has a serious problem with change. It is deathly afraid it must die to be reborn into that new consciousness. And, in fact, that's what happens during the transformation process. Once you've changed your mind about who you will be, your old way of being will cease to exist.

Understandably, your ego does not want to die, so you can expect it to resist the proposed change with all sorts of tricks for getting you back into the old box. So, step out of your box, but do so, knowing that your ego does not want you changing your mind about anything. Ego does not want you transformed.

As a result of that resistance, most people, about 85 percent of those who attempt a change of circumstances, will fizzle out in the process. That's the bad news.

The good news is: the Power Pause is your perfect tool for dealing with all the forms of ego resistance.

Ego's tricks

Ego has many tricks for getting you back into your box once you're out of it. Your ego uses fear, worry, self-doubt and mind chatter to trick you back into the old box. Mind chatter is ego's attempt to talk you back into that old box.

When you are into fear, self-doubt or worry, ego is in charge of the moment. When you take the mind chatter seriously, you are being sucked into your ego's trap. You are being your ego.

Your way out of that entrapment is to become the objective observer and use the Power Pause to escape the trap.

Any time you're upset, with fear, worry or self-doubt, the Power Pause can change your mood from negative to positive in seconds. This works because, in that moment when you become the observer, you are no longer being your ego. That's when the Real You declares a Power Pause moment.

So, what, exactly is a Power Pause?

The Power Pause is a three-step process, beginning with a moment of peace.

1. **For the first step**, you will want to remember a time and a place where you've experienced real peace— maybe on the beach in Hawaii hearing the sound of the waves rolling in, or perhaps in the woods with

birds chirping and squirrels running up and down trees.

My peaceful place was a fishing hole

On the wall behind my desk, during my business owner/managing years, hung the picture of a beautiful waterfall and the natural pond it created. Many are the times I've gone fishing there in my mind.

When stressed about a business problem, I would turn in my desk chair, face that picture, and just go fishing. Each time, I found peace, and the stress went away.

Step one for the Power Pause is a moment of peace.

2. **Step two**: Once you've created a buffer of peace between you and the stressful thought, visualize yourself already in possession and successfully enjoying life in your dream reality. Empower your vision by feeling as though you were already as successful as your new being choice could make you.

3. **Step three**: Once you've captured the good feeling that naturally comes with your being that successful, say, *"Thank you God, Universe, Spirit"* or whatever you call your higher power.

   This third step is the attitude of gratitude. In this part of the Power Pause, you will thank God, feeling truly grateful that your prayer has already been answered.

   Your true manifesting power is that "knowing feeling" –knowing that your new BEING choice is already manifested in consciousness and must soon materialize as your new reality. If you are not truly feeling grateful at this point in the process you probably haven't taken the first two steps seriously.

The Power Pause is truly a transformational tool. The transformation happens because, in the process of taking those three steps, you've changed your mind about who you are or about who you will be from now on. You've stepped out of one reality and into another by changing your perspective.

So, that's it.

The three steps again:
1. Experience the peace.
2. Visualize BEING successful and capture the good feeling that accompanies that manifestation and, then,
3. With an attitude of gratitude, thank God for answering your prayer.

The Power Pause is actually an empowered prayer

The Power Pause is a powerful prayer that works every time once you get the hang of it. The Power Pause works by changing who you are being in that instant of completing the three-step process. And by changing who you are being, you've just naturally changed what belongs with you.

To really understand how it works, you must realize that, as an individualization of God, the only true prayer is "I am." The Power Pause is your way of creating a new "I am" statement.

Go find your moment of peace:
- o Visualize the reality you want.
- o Accept it as real.
- o Choose to be the one in that success picture.

o And then thank God for having already answered your prayer.

And, last but not least, you'll want to let go and let God, as the Law of Attraction brings your new reality into manifestation.

The Power Pause for dealing with ego resistance
In addition to being a powerful tool for transforming your life and changing your circumstances, the Power Pause is your very best tool for dealing with ego resistance.

To deal with your ego's tactics for getting you back into your box, begin by paying close attention to your ego mind's chattering. As the objective observer, make it your intention to change the pattern of your thinking. Begin the process of dealing with ego's fears and negative thoughts by declaring a Power Pause.

Up until now, your ego has been in charge of your thinking 24/7. But now, your intention is to change your thinking habits, replacing negative thoughts with positive thoughts.

And listen to this: To substantially transform the quality of your life, just gradually increase the percentage of happy, joyful thoughts. How hard could that be?

Your ego's attitude about the Power Pause
> It doesn't want you being transformed.
> It does not want you doing Power Pauses.
> Your ego will strongly resist your doing the Power Pause.
> Ego will tell you that you don't have time.
> Ego will make you forget to do the Power Pause,

To overcome your ego's resistance to doing the Power Pause

➤ Get the Power Pause habit and your new habit will set you free of ego dominance.
➤ Get yourself some sort of timer as a reminder.
➤ Tie the Power Pause to another habit.

Acquiring the Power Pause habit

Unless you make up your mind right now to acquire the Power Pause habit, I can guarantee that you will forget to use it when you need it most. Without the Power Pause habit, every time your ego lays a trap for you, you will fall into it and be stuck again.

Get the habit of paying attention to your thoughts and using the Power Pause to change the pattern.

So, how do you create a new habit? I would suggest you tie it to another habit.

o Pay attention to your thoughts.
o Make it your intention to replace every negative thought with a Power Pause vision of joy and happiness.
o Decide to use the Power Pause 15 times a day until you get the habit.
o Do a Power Pause in the 30 seconds after the phone rings, before you pick up and change the outcome of that phone call.
o Do the Power Pause every time you go to the restroom.
o Do the Power Pause to create your day when you wake up in the morning.

You'll especially want to declare a Power Pause moment when you are experiencing fear, self-doubt or worry. Use the Power Pause to change your moods. You'll find, as the Power Pause habit grows, that you will be at peace the moment you say *"Power Pause."*

Credit to the creator of the Power Pause
I found the Power Pause while reading, *"The Power Pause,"* by John Harricharan. I knew I had just found the transformational tool I had been looking for. It was what I needed to make my workshops complete.

I called the author to tell him I had a problem. I said,

> *John, I've just read your book and have realized that the Power Pause is what's been missing from my workshops. I have to use it. What's it going to take to get your permission to use the Power Pause in my workshops and in a book I intend to write?*

John replied,

> *No problem, Darel. Use it as you wish.*

I've been promoting the Power Pause as a powerful transformational tool ever since. In my book, *BEING THE SOLUTION* you'll find numerous examples of the ways you can use the Power Pause in transforming your health, your wealth or your relationship problems.

But you won't truly appreciate the power in the Power Pause as a tool for changing the quality of your life, until you've read, *The Power Pause* by John Harricharan. This great book was not only "can't put it down" reading, it transformed my life, as it will yours! Buy it and read it!

22. The Powerpact

The Power of three

Transformation is the key

If you want the quality of your life to improve in some way, sorry, it can't happen until you've changed your mind about who you are. It is next to impossible to change the content of your life until you've changed the context.

What's required, if you want a change of circumstances, is your transformation in consciousness!

You are a product of what you believe, and what you have in your life, right now, is what belongs with you, like it or not. Before life can get any better for you, you'll have to change your mind about what you believe.

Once you've changed your reality concept, you will have been transformed, and therefore, what you want will come into your life, automatically and effortlessly. Of course, you won't fully believe it could be that simple until you've proven it to yourself through manifested results.

In the previous chapter, you learned about a powerful magical tool for transforming the pattern of your thinking--the Power Pause. In this chapter you'll be learning about the second most magical transformational tool we offer in the BEING Workshops—**The Powerpact.**

What is a Powerpact?

A Powerpact is a support group, formed when two or three individuals of like minds meet for the common purpose of mutual support.

The word, "Powerpact," combines two words, which together, declare the intent of Powerpact partners that they're forming a pact to support and empower each other through their individual transformations in consciousness.

But a Powerpact is much more than a support team! It is actually an awesome power source for each participant to draw upon, a greater force called into BEING by their coming together, each now tapping into the power of Spirit.

Your bible explains their remarkable increase in personal power as follows: *Where two or three are gathered together in my name, there am I in the midst of them.*

There am I

What does, *there am I in the midst of them* mean? It means the spirit of God is brought forth into presence by the coming together of a mutual support group. And, like a three-battery flashlight illumines the night with far brighter intensity than three times that of a one-battery flashlight, each individual of that Powerpact support group is made many times more powerful than before their coming together.

When two Powerpact partners add their spiritual support for the other, he or she then draws on a power source far greater than three times that of the individual.

In other words, the power of God, which is always available, but not always present in each of us, shows up as a force at hand in a Powerpact meeting. And the God power in each of them is then multiplied and amplified by their coming together. They each then are able to draw on this amplified power of the Presence.

A Powerpact meeting is a sort of spiritual awakening where spirit is present and ego is out of the picture. Once you've become aware of and accepted that Presence as part of each Powerpact meeting, you will understand why you feel so empowered after each meeting.

The transformational power in a Powerpact

The miracle of transformation will take place during your Powerpact meetings. And it will happen, because support group partners have created the space of unconditional love for each other.

You'll want to keep in mind that unconditional love is the true catalyst for change.

To change the quality of your life, you must change who you are being. But before you can get from where you are now in consciousness, to where you want to be you must make where you are now okay. Strange as it may seem, before you can change who you are being, you must first make it okay not to change.

I'm saying, you must BE where you are now and make that okay before you can move on to a higher consciousness.

Your Powerpact partners, by accepting you as you are now, with no intent to fix or change you, will have created the space for you to be here now. Only then, will you be ready to move on to something better.

The Powerpact, your way past that ego resistance
The Powerpact and the Power Pause will be your most powerful tools for dealing with ego resistance.

In your weekly Powerpact meetings you will be recharging your batteries. You'll be celebrating successes, and discussing your ego's resistance to the change you want.

Your greatest need for support will be at those times when your ego has you backed into a corner and in an emotional funk. In those down times, your Powerpact partners will be reminding you that you are not your ego, and you'll be sufficiently empowered by their support to make it past your ego's fears and self-doubts.

Your ego's reactive antics will not survive a Powerpact meeting. Your two partners in that meeting, by being objective about your ego's problems, bring the presence of Spirit to the table. Ego cannot survive in that space. When spirit enters, ego must leave.

In each Powerpact meeting, instead of three egos exchanging victim stories, you'll have three spiritually empowered individuals amplifying the Presence in each.

That's why you will be so empowered by your Powerpact meetings.

A Powerpact meeting:
- Brings into being a collective field of energy of far greater intensity than the individuals, on their own, could generate.
- Raises the power of Presence in each.
- Takes you instantly out of ego dominance and into spiritual awareness.
- Frees the group's consciousness from ego dominance.
- Creates the space for three transformations to take place.
- Grows the consciousness of each Powerpact partner.
- Gives each a giant boost in self-confidence and self-worth.
- Exponentially multiplies each partner's personal power.
- Gives each Powerpact partner a powerful model for improving the quality of all other relationships.

What a Powerpact is and what it isn't
True Powerpact support is:
- Not coaching.
- Not helping or rescuing.
- Not about fixing or changing.
- Not about problem solving, suggesting or brainstorming.
- Not about judging or opinionating.
- Not a Mastermind.
  - While a Mastermind might include all of the above, a Powerpact is none of the above.
  - A mastermind is two or more like-minded individuals who come together as a team,

intending to win the game or accomplish some common goal.

What a Powerpact is

A Powerpact is strictly a support group with no other purpose than the support of each partner in and through the process of being and becoming who he/she would BE if he or she had already manifested the chosen reality.

The intent of each Powerpact partner is to create the space for a transformation in the other two. With this in mind, each will make it his or her intention to use unconditional love as the catalyst for that change in the other two parties.

As a Powerpact partner you'll want to enter Powerpact meetings ready to listen from the heart, with full attention and no personal agenda.

The quality of your listening will let the person sharing know he or she is truly being heard and accepted as he or she is without judgment. That quality of listening is the true catalyst for his or her change.

You and your Powerpact partners will be transformed--BE and BECOME who you've each said you wanted to be—as a result of having created the sort of loving space for each other. You will be the catalyst for their transformation, as they will for you.

The art of listening

Have you ever gone to a party and just watched, with the intention of finding someone who was truly listening? Try it. It's an interesting experiment.

To God or As God

You'll find almost no one listens without some personal agenda. Generally speaking, in most conversations between friends, nobody is really home in the listening department. They're each waiting for their chance to speak.

Do you have a best friend who is always there for you, listening with no intention to fix or change you? That quality of friend is rare, indeed.

That sort of best-friend-quality listening is what you should expect from your Powerpact partners. And if you've recently joined such a group, you'll probably end up with two new best friends.

The direct benefits of BEING in a Powerpact
  o You will discover who you really are (accomplishing your true purpose in life).
  o Your personal power multiplied many times over.
  o Your support to others will empower you.
  o You will experience being truly supported by another.
  o Through their support, you'll survive those awful lows when you've felt like quitting.
  o You could end up having your life BE the way you've always wanted it.
  o The quality of all your relationships will quite naturally and exponentially improve from your having acquired new relationship skills.

Self-discovery is a gradual awakening to the reality that comes from knowing from experience, that God lives life in and through you as you. This god power in you will be awakened in you during your Powerpact meetings.

Everyone needs a Powerpact

The Powerpact is an awesome source for growing your personal power—your self-confidence and your self-worth.

If you can accept that life's true purpose is self-discovery— the seeking of self-knowledge and personal power— everyone on this planet should be in at least one Powerpact.

A support group is an essential ingredient to any successful out-of-the-box venture. In fact, no individual or company ever greatly succeeded without the empowerment that comes from Powerpact participation.

Finding suitable Powerpact partners

Success in any form is an outside-the-box experience that will always require some degree of consciousness growth. Anyone who is on a similar path of self-discovery would be a suitable Powerpact partner.

To find your Powerpact partners, attend personal growth workshops and become acquainted with likely partners for your support group.

Have lunch with likely candidates and share your intentions to grow. Their response to your sharing during that lunch will let you know if they might be potential support group partners.

How many in a Powerpact?

A Powerpact can consist of any number of people. Every winning team is a Powerpact. Two people who have come together in love and support of each other are also a Powerpact. However, two or three is the ideal Powerpact size for maximum individual support and personal growth.

To God or As God

The Bible definition for a Powerpact, often misquoted as "two or more," actually says, "two or three."

Establishing your Powerpact

- o Agree that you are suitable for one another as part of your mutual support group.
- o Agree on the place and time of your meetings.
- o Make sure each partner understands the true purpose of the Powerpact support group.
- o Review and agree on your Powerpact rules of conduct.
- o Have trial meetings before deciding for certain that you are right for each other.
- o The test: you must each feel empowered—as in liking yourself more while participating in that group.

How to BE in a Powerpact

Learning how to listen:

- Listen with your full attention,
- Lean forward, look into his/her eyes as he/she speaks. If meeting on the phone, imagine yourself face to face with him/her.
- Listen more for who he/she is BEING than to the words spoken.
- Restate what he/she said, *If I heard you right, you said....*
- Ask, *Who do you want to be listened to as?*

Ask yourself:

- o How can I help him/her to like his/herself?

What question can I ask to:

- o Help him/her see beyond that problem to its solution?
- o Help him/her see that he/she is the only solution?

- o Help him/her find his/her personal power?
- o Help him/her believe more in his/herself?

Powerpact rules of conduct

Be committed to the group consciousness.
Dedicate a regular time for your Powerpact meetings.
Honor your agreement.
- Always show up.
- Always be on time.

Be totally committed to empowering each other.
Don't confuse coaching as support--it's not the same!
- Support accepts who he/she is BEING.
- Un-requested coaching is often considered criticism.

Path to Spiriual Awakening

23. Your Money Barriers

Your Money Barrier

How to remove your barriers to having money

If monetary success eludes you, if you've ever hoped or planned for some sort of financial success that just never happened, wouldn't you like to know what sabotaged your success?

Monetary success eludes you because you have at least one built-in barrier to becoming any richer than you are now. In fact, you probably have more than one anti-rich belief that's keeping you poorer than you've wanted to be. What does a money barrier look like, and where did it come from?

Your money barrier is nothing more substantial than an assumed, erroneous point of view about:

- How money is acquired.
- What's good or bad about having lots of money.
- Those who already have money in abundance.

Your barrier

Your barrier may be any one or more of the following:

Early on in life, you bought into the idea that:

- Money is in short supply—there's never enough.
- Rich people are the bad guys.
- Rich people never live happy lives.
- Rich people don't go to heaven.
- All rich people are greedy misers.
- The only honest way to earn money is trading hours for dollars.
- Money is the root of all evil.
- The pie is only so big, and if I take a bigger piece, someone will have to do without.
- It takes money to make money.
- There will never be enough, no matter what.

Then there are also those self-concept barriers like:

- I'm not smart enough.
- I'm not good enough.
- I don't have time.
- I don't know how.

Where did that idea come from?

In growing up, you may have experienced an ongoing manifestation of your parent's point of view about money: that there never seemed to be enough of it to go around. As a child, if you bought into that lack-consciousness reality concept, that idea would still be a part of your subconscious Belief System (B.S.).

And since we must always manifest whatever we believe, and will continue to do so for as long as that hidden programming is running our life, you'll just naturally continue manifesting the reality of never having enough.

If your parents believed rich people were the bad guys, and you latched on to that dumb idea as your own, you could never, ever let yourself be one of THEM!

If your Sunday school teacher told you money was the root of all evil, you would naturally feel guilty any time you had more than enough money and you'd get rid of any surplus like it was a "hot potato." Furthermore, you would also probably feel greedy if you desired more money.

If your parents lived from paycheck to paycheck, your subconscious programming would probably have you, as a child, experiencing feeling poor along with your parents each time the money ran out before the next paycheck.

The Spender's Law of Money

People with this problem live their lives under **The Spender's Law of Money**, which says, no matter how much you make,

your expenses will always rise
to meet the level of your income.

Most of those governed by the spender's law will have the mistaken idea that being rich is just about spending the money. Because they've always wanted to be rich, they'll spend their money as soon as it comes in, feeling rich only when they're spending it.

The story goes on and on, repeating with each paycheck. Each time, when the money's all spent, they find themselves back to square one, wondering why they're always poor.

Most spenders fall into the credit card trap—that of spending their income even before it comes in. I want you to see that the real trap is **the mistaken idea that** *rich is about spending the money.*

Acquiring a prosperity consciousness
Of course, there's nothing wrong with spending money (that's what it's for). But if you ever want to BE rich, you must first acquire a prosperity consciousness. Being truly rich is not about spending or about how much you have; it is about who you are in consciousness.

A prosperity consciousness is nothing more complicated than feeling good about yourself when you think about your relationship to money. When you are feeling prosperous, you'll attract money like a magnet, and the more you have, the more prosperous you'll feel, and the more prosperous you feel, the more you'd attract. As that prosperous feeling continues to grow, your income will grow.

A negative cash flow
If you continue to spend your money as fast, or faster than you make it, you may never acquire a prosperity consciousness. Without it, you can never be rich, and it is next to impossible to feel prosperous when your cash flow is negative for any period of time. Isn't it time you changed the programming that controls your cash flow?

Remember, you arrived at your opinion about money at a time in your life when you were not old enough or wise enough to do your own thinking. Your parents' point of view about money, about rich people, and about how honest money is earned was just that—their opinion. It was just the story they made up to justify never having enough money.

Unfortunately that story became the pattern for their lives. People, including your parents, live most of their lives as their ego. And, as you know, egos have to be right about everything. People who are not rich tend to make those who have money in abundance, wrong with all the reasons they can dream up.

If you are not already rich

The sad part of your parents' story about the evils of having lots of money is that their attitude about money has now become your flawed opinion, as well.

How do I know that? If you're not already rich, you've bought into someone else's opinion about "the evils of having lots of money." If you're not already rich, it can only be because you've chosen not to be rich. Your reason for that choice will be your barrier to wealth. Wouldn't you like to find and remove your money barriers?

Finding your money barrier

If you answered yes to that question, see if you can walk yourself through all the steps of the following exercise in barrier removal. There are two ways to discover your money barrier:

1. Remember the original incident around which you built your story; allow yourself to see that your conclusion does not stand the test of logic.
2. The other way to find your barrier is to choose past it. In other words, make a solid committed decision to BE richer than you are now. Once you've chosen your money goal, your barrier will pop up to stand between you and your becoming rich. Deal with it then.

Your Money Barriers

A barrier removal exercise:

First, know that some erroneous assumption made early on in life now stands between you and financial independence.

- o That's your erroneous conclusion about money
- o That's the idea that's keeping you poorer than you've wanted to be
- o You've staked the quality of your life on that belief

1. Realize that the conclusion arrived at back then, once uncovered, does not stand the test of logic (that's why your ego has hidden it).
2. Then ask yourself if you're willing to let some silly, nonsensical reason stand between you and the good life you want?
3. Choose to uncover and examine the validity of your reason for choosing to be poor.
4. Now, look at the change you want in your life.
5. Ask yourself who you would be BEING if that change were already realized.
6. Imagine your life as it would be if you were that rich.
7. Then, choose to BE that rich.
8. Then, as a result of that BEING choice, listen to your ego's reactive self-talk.
9. What fears are showing up as a result of your choice?
10. What's the belief behind those fears?
11. Would you bet the rest of your life on that belief?

If not, make up you mind to replace that erroneous conclusion with something that would serve you better. If you're brave enough, today, and if your self-worth will allow it, you'll choose to be richer. Then you'll uncover and take a long hard look at what's keeping you stuck in the status quo of insufficient income.

Why Have A Coach?

Why you may need a coach

You've just learned the secret to the good life. You've just discovered that you are far more powerful than you've ever imagined. But you've had this power all your life and didn't have a clue.

You are a god with the tendency to have amnesia from time to time. You'll need a coach who will help you remember your True Identity.

You have a powerful ego that will be as determined to get you back into the old box as you are to stay out and manifest your dream reality.

Without a coach, your ego will have just created a bigger box out of your new reality concept and you will, once again, be trapped in that box. A coach will help you keep thinking outside the box.

Why Have A Coach?

With a coach, you'll have a far better chance to keep the Real You, that Spirit of Aliveness and Enthusiasm in you, in charge of your life. That IS your intention, isn't it?

As you now know, one of ego's favorite stories is, *But I don't know how! -- How can it happen if I don't know how to make happen?*

It's not your job to know how.

Your job is to make the BEING commitment and to know that the Universe will reveal the "how to," and then you'll just take whatever inspired action shows up for you to take. You know the "how to" will show up in the form of opportunities, and you'll be enthusiastically responding to those opportunities as they show up with, *Yes, Yes,* and, *Yes.*

Of course, your greatest barrier to having life be this simple will be your attachment to the idea that you have to make it happen. If the truth were known, you've got your identity tied into, *if it's going to be it's up to me.*

To get yourself past that built-in success barrier, you must give up your make-it-happen identity in favor of the easy way to manifest success. A good "BEING" coach will lead you with questions through the letting-go process.

You know, in theory, that all you have to do is choose the results you want, make the appropriate BEING commitment, and then turn the delivery job over to the Universe.

Ego doesn't want you to know

Your ego doesn't want you to know life is that simple; so, to amp up your manifesting powers, you'll need to focus on increasing three things:

To God or As God

1. Your faith in the process.
2. Your belief in yourself.
3. Your ability to accept—your self-worth.

You know now that your ability to choose an out-of-the-box goal is not a measure of what the Universe can deliver; instead, it's a measure of what your self-worth will allow you to accept. For the Universe, there is no limit to the supply.

The limit in place is the one you've set on what you can allow yourself to accept.

The only way to increase your belief in yourself and the unfailing power of principle is by proving it to yourself with out-of-the-box baby steps that each becomes your manifested reality. Your consciousness, your self-confidence, and your self-worth will grow with each successful trip out of the box.

The only problem with the idea of frequent trips out of the box is that your powerful ego is determined to give you amnesia about the time you successfully settle into your newly manifested reality.

You'll probably forget

Without a BEING coach, you will forget that you have the power, and it may be two or more years before you become disenchanted enough to rebel and choose again. Without a coach, you'll reach the next level and quit. A good BEING coach would keep you out of that ego trap.

Your true purpose in life is self discovery, and the Game of Life is set up so that the growing cycle is a repeating process.

Why Have A Coach?

With each step up the grand stairway of self-discovery (growing your consciousness) you'll have an excitingly awesome new perspective on life. Each step up in consciousness will feel like this is home or your final destination. It isn't.

Life is a journey, not a destination. Your ego doesn't agree. When your ego takes over, once again, you are back in the box—a bigger box, but it's still a box. You'll need a coach to keep you growing and out of the box. Let's face it: life is a daring adventure or it is not. Don't let your ego decide for you. Hire yourself a coach.

A big part of mastering your life is about conquering your fears. That doesn't mean the fears will ever be totally gone, never to show up again. You'll always have an ego, and as you continue growing your consciousness, your ego will be threatened by those changes.

You'll be the master, in charge of your life, as long as you are not controlled by your fears.

Your ego's survival job

Ego is your survival mechanism. Its primary job is survival. Fear is your ego's early warning system alerting you to a possible danger. You'll never want to stop listening to your ego. There'll be times when its fears will be justified. At those times, if you act quickly, you'll probably avoid a mishap.

Unfortunately, most of ego's fears are based on its fear of change and the threat to your survival won't be real. If you are like most people, you are confined to your old box by those fears.

But maybe you're out of your box—growing your consciousness—that sets you above the crowd.

To be the master, you'll need three primary missions
1. Grow your consciousness—becoming more and more consciously aware of your True Identity
2. Take back the controls--every day increasing the percentage of time the Real You is in charge
3. Totally understanding and learning how to deal with your ego's tricks for getting you back into the old box

Your ego's job in life is to provide you with the experience of life as you have perceived it to be in your current reality concept. When ego takes over that role, its tendency is to totally take over the running of your life.

But ego is your servant, not your master. To take back the controls and be master of your life, you must put the Real You in charge. Take a long hard look at the three intentions above and ask yourself if you can really accomplish your mission without the guidance of good BEING coach.

Your need for a coach
Check off the tools you're using regularly ✔
1. Facing your fears- ....yes __ no __
Need coaching __
2. Making it okay to fail .... yes __ no __
Need coaching __
3. Renegotiating agreements with others... yes __ no __
Need coaching __
4. Talking to your ego—reassuring it ..:.:.. yes __ no __
Need coaching __
5. I am not my ego .... yes __ no __
Need coaching __
6. Positive evidence journal .... yes __ no __
Need coaching __

Why Have A Coach?

7. The Power Pause ....   yes __ no __
    Need coaching __
8. Your Powerpact support group ....   yes __ no __
    Need coaching __
9. ....   yes __ no __
    Need coaching __
10. ....   yes __ no __
    Need coaching __

Now it's your turn again
What have your learned so far?

Part IV Mastering Your Life

Congratulations!

Your Life With Spirit In Charge

As the true master of your life, you will be:
- Easily maintaining a stress-less winner's attitude at all times.
- A magnet for attracting whoever and whatever you wanted in life.
- Creating and manifesting new realities at will, but your true mission will be to make a difference in the lives of others.
- Easily dealing with any ego resistance.
- Living in the joy.
- Totally present to life, living in the now.
- Healthy, wealthy, and rich in loving relationships.
- Having more than enough free time to enjoy your life, your family and your money.
- Practicing unconditional love in all relationships.
- Super self confident. Your consciousness and your self-worth will have grown beyond the need to prove anything to yourself or anyone else.
- Not attached to any of your material manifestations.

Are you ready to take charge?

Becoming a true master of your life can only begin for you after you've made a solid and total commitment to BEING the one in charge of your life. And since you are an individualization of God, this means you will become a master at dealing with life AS a god in all aspects of your life.

Once you've begun to understand the true nature of God, and have become powerful, a god in your own life, you'll be practicing the presence in all areas of your life.

The power of God in you is passive power, the power to choose who you will BE, not the power to make things happen. In practicing at BEING god, you will practice ways of BEING that make you a powerful magnet for attracting success in all ways, including health, wealth and relationships.

The following list will give you some idea about what you will be practicing on your way toward becoming the master.

In mastering your life you will:

- o Have acquired a winner's attitude by making failure your friend.
- o Be growing your confidence, your self-worth and your consciousness, exercising your manifesting powers by making frequent out-of-the-box BEING choices.
- o Be more and more certain that when you make a committed BEING choice, it must always manifest.
- o Easily detach from the status quo before making a new BEING choice.
- o Become a master at dealing with ego's fear-based survival traps.

- o Practice unconditional love in all your relationships.

To God or As God

- Apply unconditional love to the art of listening to your significant other, your kids, and prospects/customers.
- BE present for whatever is happening, living in the now.
- Be going for the joy, living in the joy.

If you are truly ready to take over the controls and become Master of Your Life, you might want to write the following commitments on a 4x6 card and repeat daily, until you've memorized and solidified your intention.

I hereby commit to:

1. Growing my consciousness through daily demonstrations of my manifesting powers, becoming more and more consciously aware of my True Identity with each manifested result.
2. Becoming a true master in the art of dealing with my ego's manipulative tricks for getting me back into the old box.
3. Practicing BEING present as the observer, taking charge, more every day, ever-increasing the percentage of time the Real Me, not my ego, is in charge of my life.

Signed, _____

Date_____

And, now, that you're committed, how does that feel? Are you already feeling more powerful, more in charge?

Mastering Your Life Skills

1. Acquiring the winning attitude by making it okay to fail.
2. As you grow in consciousness, you'll be renegotiating agreements with others.
3. Keeping a positive evidence journal.
4. Living in the Now with your NOW clock on your desk.

5. Getting out of your act—uncovering your hidden fear—so you can be real.
6. Creating the space of unconditional love in all situations.

Part IV chapters

 <u>Now it's your turn again</u>

What have your learned so far?

25. Practicing The Presence

Having god-like powers will have very little value for you, in terms of changing the quality of your life, until you've begun to assume the role of a god. You've always been an individualization of God, and you've always had the power of a god, but where has it gotten you?

You've spent most of your life stuck in the status quo, because you've been living your life as your ego. But now you know that's not who you are.

You've rediscovered your power and chosen out of your box many times in your life. But you've done so without realizing the power you were using was the power of God operating in and through you as the BEING Principle.

As a god, all your thoughts are BEING choices, and that means all your thoughts are powerful prayers that must be answered by a Universe that always says, "Yes," but never

Practicing The Presence

"No." Your life is not about becoming more powerful; you already are powerful beyond your wildest dreams.

To increase your ability to manifest grand results at will, you'll first want to take responsibility for what you are already creating. It should be obvious to you by now, that in order to experience BEING powerful, you must take charge of both your thoughts and your attitudes.

In the process of taking charge, you'll become more aware that a simple change of attitude can change the quality of your life. In effect, you'll be learning how to pray and "how to think as a god." And believe me; that change in your thinking habits will take a lot of practice.

You'll be replacing bad habits with good ones. Think of your new role in life as "practicing the presence."

Unless you've grown in consciousness far beyond the average, your ego is now in charge of your thoughts and your emotions 99 percent of the time. And, with ego running your life, you've been on an emotional roller coaster.

To escape that up-one-day, down-the-next emotional ride you'll be putting the Real You in charge of your attitudes and your thoughts.

In case you were wondering why ego, not spirit, is running your life, it's because perhaps, until now, you were not aware of your ego, and you've never actually chosen to BE the one in charge. Up until now, you probably haven't realized you were not your ego.

But now that you know, you'll be choosing to BE the one in charge. Your new BEING choice, to BE the one in charge, will require a transformation in consciousness, and that will be the most important decision of your life.

Transformation simply means you've changed your mind about who you are and who you will be. A transformation is nothing more complicated than a change in your point of view or your attitude about life. And your new reality is created by simply changing the pattern of your thinking.

Think of your life, with ego in charge, as just an unhealthy thinking habit—your habitual way of thinking, reacting and being.

But now you that intend to put spirit in charge, you'll be creating some new thinking habits. In effect, by stepping out of the ego role and into the BEING mode, you'll be being a god in your own life. To get clear about what you're up to in this take-over process, you might want to call it, "practicing the presence."

Everything new that ever happened in your life began with an intention, a BEING choice, and it ended in manifesting some form of consequence.

If you are not happy with the emotional ups and downs or the circumstances you've created, you'll want to make that new BEING choice now. Simply choose to BE the one in charge.

The task of taking charge of your life is simply a matter of managing your BEING choices, moment by moment. Before you can do that, you must choose and be committed to BEING the one in charge. Taking charge is simply a BEING choice.

Practicing The Presence

Why take charge?

Realize it or not, all your attitudes, opinions, and points of view, and all your thoughts are actually BEING choices. In fact, you are so powerful right now that all your thoughts are prayers and all your prayers are answered.

The problem is you haven't been the one in charge of your thoughts. Instead, your ego has been doing the thinking almost 24/7, and your manifested results are the effect of ego's BEING choices.

In taking over the controls, your job as spirit is to replace your ego as the one in charge of your thinking and your life.

That may seem like a big deal, but it's not. Think of the job of replacing ego with spirit as similar to that of exercising a muscle. You don't have to take total charge of your whole life right now; you just choose, from moment to moment, to take charge of that moment. In the process, you'll be creating a new BEING habit.

The more you intentionally use your power to BE, the more powerful you will become.

You will be practicing the presence by:

- o Thinking outside the box.
- o Being in the creative mode.
- o Being the observer.
- o Being totally present for another, practicing unconditional love.
- o Being a good listener.
- o Being objective, talking to your ego.
- o Being totally present to whatever's happening in the now.
- o Being enthusiastic.

To God or As God

- o Living in the joy of the moment.
- o Being grateful.
- o Choosing to be happy.
- o Doing a Power Pause moment.
- o Appreciating beauty.
- o Enjoying a moment of peace.

Review this list daily with the intention of choosing to make each one of those skills a natural habit.

There are those who believe the knowledge that you are an individualization of God suddenly makes you more powerful. Sorry. Knowing that truth, in and of itself, doesn't change anything. That power, like electricity, doesn't do anything for you until you've plugged it in and turned it on.

The power of God in you is a power you've always had. It's called "The BEING Principle." The problem isn't that you haven't had the power, but from ignorance, you've been using your power to focus on and perpetuate your problems. As your ego, you would be living in the past with guilt, or in the future with fear. As Spirit, you will be living in the present-in the now.

When ego is in charge
When ego is in charge, you will live your life in the survival mode, mostly reactive or inactive, dormant and stagnant. As your ego, your motivation in life is fear, self-doubt and worry. Because all your decisions come out of fear and worry, they are reactive and defensive.

As Spirit, you will be enthusiastic, joyful and happy. Your motivation will be a powerful desire for further growth in consciousness. All your decisions will be proactive, exciting and out of the box, made with a winner's attitude as you anticipate the thrill of your next daring adventure.

Taking charge

If your life is a living hell of fear and self-doubt, the idea of BEING a god may seem far-fetched and out of the question, but it is not: Taking charge of your life is merely a matter of taking charge of the moment. Actually, it's a simple process of paying attention to your thoughts and feelings, choosing a different attitude for the moment.

When you are into fear, worry, or self-doubt, you are BEING your ego. To put the Real You in charge, just step back from the situation and BE the observer. Once you've taken an objective view as the observer, your ego is no longer in control. What a simple way to practice BEING present!

Practicing the Presence is nothing more complicated than living in the NOW. You'll find a whole chapter devoted to the subject of "Living In The Now."

Paying attention

Ego's constant survival thoughts are called "mind chatter." As the observer, you'll want to pay close attention to that self-talk. You've been given several powerful tools for dealing with your ego's fear-based antics. Talk to your ego. When you're talking to your ego, you can't BE your ego.

Any time your emotions turn negative with fear or self-doubt, declare a Power Pause moment. The Power Pause changes who you are being at that moment and automatically changes the outcome of the next moment. You'll find nothing more powerful than the Power Pause for putting the Real You in charge of the moment.

To be a winner in the Game of Life, you must acquire the winner's attitude. With the attitude of a winner, you will have made a friend of failure. As a winner, you'll know you may experience failure many times in your lifetime, but for you a temporary failure is just a bump in the road. After each of those learning experiences, you'll end up more powerful. As a winner, you'll know failure as a friend.

As a winner

As a winner, you'll know the little-known truth about life: no one ever wins until they've made it okay to fail. And with the winner's attitude, you'll know you can't lose because you won't quit when you stub your toe and fall. You'll just get off your knees and take off again. You have become a winner, because you are no longer afraid of failure.

As a winner, you'll know your word is law in the Universe; every word you speak and every thought you think is a prayer. And because the Universe knows only how to say "yes," all your prayers are answered.

So, anytime you find yourself manifesting what you don't want, you'll be changing your BEING choice.

You'll know for certain that when you make a solid, focused BEING commitment, your new reality must manifest. To take charge of manifesting the results you want, you'll be changing how you speak and the way you think.

The power of God in you is passive, proactive power. It is the power to choose who you will BE. Once you've chosen, the Universe must deliver on that choice. The BEING Principle in you makes you all powerful to the degree that you become aware of that power and grow more certain of your manifesting powers.

The true nature of God

The true nature of God is love—unconditional love. So, to grow your God powers, you'll want to practice creating the space of unconditional love in all relationships, especially as it relates to the art of listening.

As ego, your tendency is to become attached to whatever you've created. As Spirit, you detach, thereby creating the space for your next BEING choice. Once your ego buys into and accepts your new reality, it will maintain that reality to the exclusion of all others.

To create the space for your next out-of-the-box adventure, you must first detach from the status quo. The chapter for detaching is called Unloading Your Camel.

In review, practicing the presence is:

- Acquiring the winner's attitude by making failure your friend.
- Growing your confidence and your consciousness as you exercise your manifesting powers—making frequent out-of-the-box BEING choices.
- Becoming more and more certain that when you make a committed BEING choice, it must always manifest.
- Easily detaching from whatever you've created.
- Becoming a master at dealing with ego's fear-based survival traps.
- Practicing unconditional love in all your relationships.
- Applying unconditional love to the art of listening.
- Learning to BE present for whatever is happening, and living in the now.
- Going for the joy, and living in the joy.

First Unload Your Camel

According to our Christian bible, Christ is reported to have said,

It is easier for a camel to go through the eye of a needle, than for a rich man to enter the Kingdom of God.

And since a live camel, quite obviously, could not possibly pass through the eye of a sewing needle, one would assume if he took that metaphor literally, a rich man could not possibly enter the kingdom. But that's not what Christ meant, not at all!

You might want to stop using the camel metaphor as your excuse for choosing not to be rich.

Unloading Your Camel

Christ was not really telling us rich people don't go to heaven, or riches are evil and rich people are the bad guys.

His metaphor had an entirely different meaning at the time He said that—a meaning far different than what we've been led to believe by those who've misinterpreted it. What did He mean?

Here's my interpretation:

But before you read my interpretation, you might want to think about something else Christ said.

He said, *the kingdom of God is within us*; so the *entering of the kingdom,* referred to in His famous metaphor must point to a state of consciousness—a spiritual awakening— rather than a place we may hope to go when we die.

To truly understand the intent of this metaphor, you'll need another meaning for *the eye of a needle*. Here's what that meant back then:

> Over 2000 years ago, when Christ walked on this earth, some ancient cities had an outer and an inner wall. The inner wall was a security measure, a way to keep beggars, pickpockets and thieves out of the inner city.

To enter into the inner city, (the kingdom) one had to pass through a small guarded opening, shaped like the eye of a needle, an opening so small a rich man's fully loaded camel could not be taken through. So, if you had lived as a rich man in the time of Christ and wanted your pet camel with you in the inner city, you would have had to, first, unload your camel.

You are that rich man

That metaphor takes on a whole new meaning, now doesn't it? If *the kingdom* refers to your spiritual awakening, and if entering *the kingdom* required the unloading of riches off your camel, then Christ's camel metaphor speaks to all of us, not just rich men.

What? You don't think you're rich? Read on: your riches are defined by whatever and to what you've become attached. The shape of your own riches may even look like poverty, if that's the reality concept to which you've become attached.

The problem is we're SO attached to our current reality concept and our way of BEING, we're not willing to give them up. Let's face it, for the moment, that's who you are! Think about it. You could have your whole identity tied up in your victim story!

Is this the load on your camel?

Take a look at some of the ideas to which you may have attached yourself:
  o Your poverty consciousness.
  o Your victim story.
  o The relationship that's not serving you.
  o The job you don't like.
  o Your anger.
  o Your resentment.

So maybe YOU are the rich man in Christ's camel metaphor and something like the above is the load on your camel's back. If so, that's your riches! This puts a whole new light on the subject of riches, doesn't it?

Unloading Your Camel

Wow! And all this time, you thought rich people were the bad guys!

Another part of the load
Of course, that's not all: You may also be attached to:
- *I'm not good enough.*
- *I'm not smart enough.*
- *I'm not old enough.*
- *I'm too old.*
- *I don't know how.*
- *It's too hard.*
- *There's never enough.*

For as long as you remain attached to any silly idea like those above, you are a rich man or woman who may not enter the kingdom!

Face it! That bible quote was meant for you and me!
- You and I are attached to the way it is--the status quo.
- We're attached to our current reality concept.
- We're attached to our way of BEING.

You must first unload your camel
You can have whatever you want from life if you can find the courage to step outside that box and choose it. But first you must believe there's a way out, and there is! Your way out is a spiritual awakening, but you won't be entering the kingdom with a loaded camel.

You won't be having what you want without first giving up your attachment to not having it. If this sounds like a catch-22 situation, it is!
- It is not possible to choose out until you believe there's a way out.

- o Even if you truly believe there's a way out, you won't be entering the kingdom because your camel is loaded with garbage.

It's a good thing you read the first part of this book and learned the way out before you read this chapter. Otherwise you wouldn't feel inclined toward unloading your camel.

But before we talk about removing the load on your camel, let's talk about why you may, first, want to seek a spiritual awakening.

Your spiritual awakening
We all want something from life that we don't have, but we can't have it because we haven't created the space for that transformation. Unloading your camel creates the space for that transformation. Your passkey to freedom is to remember that you have the power to choose out.

Christ said, *Seek ye first the kingdom, and all else will be added unto you.* With this metaphor I'm sure He intended to inform us that the only path to having life get any better begins with a spiritual awakening.

And of course, the camel metaphor suggests you won't be entering the kingdom with your camel fully loaded. Having what you want will require a change in the way you are BEING, and that won't really happen until you are ready to give up your attachment to who you are BEING now.

So, the question is:
Are you ready to give up BEING who you are now in favor of who you must BE in order to have your life the way you've always wanted it? Are you ready to unload your camel so you can enter the kingdom?

Unloading Your Camel

You think you want that better life, but you're actually very much attached to not having it. You want out of that box, but from inside the box, as your ego, you can't choose out.

Remember, the load on your camel is whatever foolish idea you're hanging on to that prevents you moving on to the next plateau. Your fear of losing what you have has you trapped. Before you can have what you want, you must first give up your attachment to not having it.

Unload your camel exercise:

Imagine standing outside the kingdom, ready to enter. You are at the wall to the inner city, observing the very small opening shaped like the *eye of a needle*. You want to take your favorite camel with you into the inner city, but the opening is far too small for your loaded camel to enter.

It is quite obvious to you that must unload your camel before you can enter the inner city.

You can hear beautiful music and joyful sounds inside the wall. You know peace, love and joy awaits you beyond that inner wall, so you finally make up your mind to unload your camel and enter.

Review: what's the load on YOUR camel?
- o   You and I are attached to the way it is--the status quo.
- o   We're attached to our current concept of reality.
- o   We're attached to our way of BEING.

You are attached to
- o   Your self-doubts.
- o   "I'm not good enough or smart enough.
- o   The idea that there is never enough.
- o   Your victim story.

Are you ready to unload that garbage?

In your hands you find a black plastic garbage bag, into which you will discard your load. One by one, you remove the items off your camel, putting each attachment into the bag. Once your camel is fully unloaded, you will be throwing that garbage bag into the dumpster next to the opening.

Review the lists of self-limiting ideas you found in the first part of this chapter. Make some notes identifying which ideas are part of the load on your camel, and then list below what you will unload.

_____ .

_____ .

_____ .

_____ .

_____ .

_____ .

_____ .

_____ .

Now that you've taken the load off your camel, how does that feel? Do you:

- o Feel lighter?
- o Free?
- o Energized?
- o _____ .
- o _____ .
- o _____ .
- o _____ .
- o _____ .

Tie the bag and throw it in the dumpster. Then take the reins and lead your camel into the kingdom.

Unloading Your Camel

You've entered the kingdom and had a spiritual awakening. Experience the peace, the joy, the happiness. And now, while in the space of power, enlightenment and enthusiasm, choose your next out-of-the-box adventure.

Now it's your turn

What's your greatest 'ah ha' so far?

27. Being The Lighthouse

The Power to BE

The Power to Attract

Two awesome powers

As an individualization of God you have two awesome powers working almost magically to bring into your life whatever belongs with you. Those two powers are the Power to BE and the Power to Attract. You've been using those two amazing powers all your life without a clue that you had any real power.

And you've been attracting what? I'll bet that the "what" you've been attracting is not the "what" you've really wanted. Maybe now is the time for you learn how to attract who and what you REALLY want.

Is it that time for you, yet?

After 15 years of working 12 to 14 hours a day, running a business with over 100 employees, I finally woke up to the fact that life was passing me by. The dawning came during a two-week golfing vacation in Hawaii.

Back from that trip, I decided it was time to stop being a workaholic; it was time to back off and begin to enjoy life and spend more time with my family.

The interesting thing about my semi-retirement decision was that I already had the key people in place. I just hadn't given them the full responsibilities that belonged with their jobs as production manager, sales manager and office manager.

I expected a loss in volume
As a make-it-happen boss, I assumed the business would suffer in volume loss as a result of my reduced hours. I was prepared to accept that consequence. But what really happened was a giant blow to my ego. My net profits tripled.

It was then that I realized my success in business had not been the make-it-happen phenomenon I had believed it was. Instead, my business success had been the result of a series of BEING choices and my willingness to accept that success as it showed up--success delivered automatically by a Universe that only knows how to say, "Yes."

My job as CEO of my company was simply to maintain our long-term vision goal and support my key people in their BEING and DOING decisions. With this entirely different approach to managing my business, I could easily get the job done by working four hours a day instead of fourteen.

And how about you?
You might want to consider this example from my life and ask yourself if you're making the same mistake I did? Are you getting too big a bang out of being a make-it-happen manager to let go and let the Universe deliver? Are you too attached to making it happen?

To God or As God

Contrary to what most of us have believed, the power of God in us is not a make-it-happen sort of power—it's a passive power—the power to choose who you will BE. Once you've chosen, the power of attraction automatically clicks in to bring you whatever belongs with that BEING choice.

Once you've accepted the idea that success is a BEING choice, you'll choose the let-it-happen path to success; you'll get twice the results with half the effort. Wouldn't that be a reason to let go of your make-it-happen approach to life?

Can you give up that idea?
Of course, I realize what a sacrifice it would be for you to give up on the idea that you're too busy making it happen to let go and let the Universe deliver. I know what a blow that is to the ego, because I've been there—done that!

Whether you know it or not, you are already a magnet, a powerful force for attracting what belongs with you. The secret to attracting what you want is to first get clear about what you want. Then imagine who you would be "BEING" if you already had it. Once you've chosen to BE that person, the Universe is obliged to deliver the appropriate content.

An example of how this works
In my early years of learning business management skills the hard way, my hiring procedure was naive and ineffective. I'd put an ad in the paper, such as, "SALESMAN WANTED," interview all day, then hire the person I liked best.

Next, I would foolishly attempt to train that person in the necessary skills for the job.

One day, I wised up to this realization: I should be hiring people who were already qualified for the job. Duh! Then, before placing the ad, I'd spend considerable time writing a job description, listing necessary skills the applicant must have to apply. I placed the ad only when I was clear about what I wanted.

As before, I interviewed all day and hired the best person for the job, but I almost never hired someone who responded to the ad in the paper. Instead, almost invariably, the right person for the job was someone who had not seen the ad. He or she just walked in off the street.

This happened far too often to be considered a mere coincidence. It finally dawned on me what was happening. Once clear about who I wanted for the job, the Universe filled the order by sending me the right person for that job.

One more example

When my regular massage therapist took a day off, I called Kelly to ask if she was available as a substitute. She was, and when I arrived at her place of business, I asked how she was doing.

She replied, *I don't know if you know this, Darel, but I've been out of business for over five months. I had a car accident and couldn't use my hands.*

I responded, *I didn't know that, Kelly. How are you doing?* I repeated the question, *how's business.*

She said, *You're the first. I just today started back in business, but it's going to be okay. I'll just get on the phone and start calling people.*

To God or As God

I suggested, *Kelly, what if I could show you an easier way—a way to attract, rather than prospect for customers?*

She was really interested. I explained the Lighthouse Exercise to her. Then I asked if she would be willing to do the exercise several times a day until her schedule filled. She agreed.

The next time I saw Kelly, two weeks later, I asked again, *How's business?*

She said, *You won't believe this, Darel, but I lack only one client in filling my week's schedule.*

That's incredible, Kelly! I said. *I'm not at all surprised it worked, but I'm amazed that you were able to fill your schedule so quickly. How do you explain that?*

Kelly answered, *I already understood the principle from the times I heard you speak at Toastmasters.*

Later, in reviewing her process, I wondered how she had been able to manifest that many clients so quickly. I realized two things:

- o Five months earlier, prior to doing the Lighthouse Exercise, Kelly had already been very successful as a massage therapist. She didn't have to wonder who she would have to be to fill the shoes of a successful massage therapist.
- o She didn't have to wonder or be afraid that she couldn't handle the business once her schedule filled.

In other words, she didn't have any of the usual self-doubts most people would have after setting a goal. Kelly could easily and comfortably step back into the role of BEING successful as a massage therapist.

Synchronicity

As a principle of life, the Law of Attraction automatically brings into our lives everything naturally belonging in the reality of our BEING choices. One of the most frequently observed examples of this law in action is, *Synchronicity*.

If you've ever answered the door or the phone knowing who was calling before you opened the door or picked up the phone, you've experienced synchronicity. Synchronicity works because each of us humans send out a sort of radar beam that automatically attracts whoever and whatever belongs with us.

This awesome attraction power brings us who and whatever belongs in our lives because we humans are all subliminally interconnected. We are in tune with one another in ways of which we are seldom aware. We are just naturally more in synch with those to whom we feel closest.

Strategic synchronicity

Even though not consciously aware of the phenomenon of *synchronicity*, we humans just naturally attract who and what belongs with us. We also attract those who need and want what we are willing and ready to offer.

Those who belong in your life have already shown up. They are your friends, prospects, clients and customers. Once you understand the awesome power of strategic synchronicity, you'll be using it systematically and intentionally to attract who and whatever you want into your life.

To God or As God

You've heard about spiritual marketing? This is that process in a nutshell. If you are in a business that depends on a steady supply of clients and customers, you'll want to be using synchronicity as your way of attracting them. This form of subliminal communication is in effect at all times.

The Lighthouse Exercise

To strategically attract clients, prospects and customers, you'll be doing what we call the Lighthouse Exercise. Read the sample script below for the exercise. You can also visit beingsolution.com and listen to it as an audio message.

A lighthouse stands tall in one place, strong and centered, sending out a powerful beam of light as a beacon representing a harbor of safety for all boats. A lighthouse does not uproot itself and run frantically up and down the beach attempting to gather in all the boats. It stands firm, as an always-present guide for attracting boats looking for a safe harbor. It doesn't worry about boats with a different destination.

The Lighthouse Exercise

As part of the exercise, you'll want to list the qualities you expect to find in your perfect prospect, customer or client. Below are a few suggestions:

The perfect customer:
- Is friendly and easy to deal with.
- Always keeps appointments.
- Calls in plenty of time if he or she can't make it.
- Always shows up on time.
- Is a repeat customer.
- Can afford your service and is ready to pay.
- Is loyal to you.
- Refers friends to you.
- _____(add some of your own)

o _____

Now that you know what makes the perfect customer, the next question is, "Who would you be BEING if you were attracting that perfect customer?"
Here's another list:

You'd have to be

- o Friendly and easy to deal with.
- o A great listener.
- o Always reliable.
- o Always give two weeks notice if you can't keep the appointment.
- o Always on time or a little early.
- o Ready to put the customer's needs before your own.
- o Truly grateful for referrals.
- o _____(add some of your own)
- o _____
- o _____

Now, you'll want to choose to BE that person and do the following exercise:

Getting centered

To do the exercise, you'll first want to get centered in your body. Close your eyes, take a deep breath and let it out slowly. Relax, and do it again. Take another deep breath and let it out slowly.

As you breath out, let go of the cares of the moment, and put all the day's problems in a garbage bag. Imagine throwing them into the trash. Just let go of your problems, focusing on being here now, and allow yourself to connect with your inner power and just BE present in the moment.

To God or As God

With your feet flat on the floor, wriggle your toes, sit back in your chair, waggle your back and get comfortable in your seat. Allow yourself to become consciously aware of your body. Stretch your arms out wide to the side, let out a big sigh, and then reach for the sky and stretch again.

Now, rotate your head on your shoulders and allow your neck to relax. With your eyes still closed, and without moving your head, look up. This sends a message to your brain that you're about to send it new information. And now, with your eyes still closed, look forward.

Imagine yourself being a lighthouse. You are standing tall on the shore of a harbor for small boats. You are standing firmly in one spot, not moving from side-to-side, not waving your arms to attract attention.

You're standing where you always stand, your beacon of light shining brightly so they'll always know how to find their way into the harbor-the haven of safety that you represent.

Think of yourself as the source of their needs, knowing that your light shines brighter because you are the giver, the source; you are not coming from need. Clients and customers who want what you have are filling your schedule every day. You don't need them. They need you.

You are BEING the source, the giver, attracting those who are in need of your services. You are BEING the person who HAS what your prospects, clients and customers want.

So now, as the lighthouse, notice storm clouds gathering-big, heavy ominous clouds. The sky is getting darker by the minute. The sea is rough, far too rough out there for small boats, and it's getting even worse.

Being The Lighthouse

Because of those rough seas and dark skies, you know those little boats need you more than ever. Those little boats seek the calmer waters of the inner harbor.

Those small boats need not fear, for you are the lighthouse, standing tall. You send out a powerful beacon of light, a welcoming message to all who see your light. And those boats move toward the haven of safety you represent.

The boats are a symbol for your customers, clients and prospects. They are in desperate need for what you have to offer.

Who you are being creates an invisible radar beam, sending a clear message to any and all who seek you and what you offer. Their needs match perfectly with what you have for them.

Now, more than enough clients happily fill your schedule every day. Those new clients are showing up because they got the message you're sending out. They were tuned in waiting to hear from you. Expect your phone to start ringing.

And now, mission complete, open your eyes and notice that you are feeling a great sense of personal power. By merely choosing a new way of BEING YOU, you have set the wheels in motion for manifesting a great new success for your business.

As a result, you now feel an awesome sense of personal power the likes of which you've never experienced before.

28

Once You're Committted

Committed

Once you are committed

Once you've truly committed yourself to a new way of being you, you've created the space for miracles. For, in that moment of your commitment, the Universe will step forward to provide all manner of circumstances, assistance and opportunities—seeming miracles that might not have occurred, otherwise.

The space for miracles

On our first group call for a BEING Workshop, it is not unusual to have a participant report that miracles happened as soon as he or she signed up for the workshop. This is a very natural result of your being committed, because once you've committed the Universe always says, "Yes," never "No."

Results could happen that quickly for you, but the speed of the Universe's delivery will depend on the level of your commitment and the degree of your certainty.

The four elements of total commitment
Four things will have happened in your moment of total commitment:
1. You will have complete and total faith in the power of principle (the BEING Principle, and the Attraction Principle).
2. You will have had a spiritual awakening, and grown your consciousness.
3. Your self-confidence will have increased.
4. You will have raised the bar on your self-worth.

Your total commitment to a new way of BEING YOU would indicate that you have all four of the above elements of your next consciousness transformation in place. With each of your steps up in consciousness, you will have increased your manifesting powers.

So what's missing?
As you think seriously about the change you want, ask yourself if you have all four elements in place. If so, you are truly committed, and the Universe is primed and ready to respond to that commitment!

For example, let's say you've been working hard all your life, trying to get ahead, but have gotten nowhere because you believe, in order to have more money, you'd have to work harder, more hours or get a second job.

And since those options are not acceptable solutions to your money problems, you're stuck in the situation of never having enough money to cover all the bases.

But now you've read most of this book and have become a believer in principle. You now know you are a part of the one god—a god individualized in you as you. You've thought about how great life would be if you were wealthy and you're ready to commit.

Know that it is a done deal

In that moment of your total commitment to BEING wealthy, the Universe will begin to bring you opportunities in the form of wealth-building investment possibilities:

- o You might get a raise in pay, which you'd decide to invest rather than spend.
- o You might have an opportunity to save on your expenses, and have even more money to invest.
- o Your newly acquired prosperity consciousness would bring you ever-increasing income.

Of course you'd have to say, "Yes" to those opportunities as they showed up. But all that IS happening is as a result of your having chosen to be wealthy. That's the way it works, and it IS as simple as that.

The question is, *Are you ready to commit to BEING wealthy?*

Wealthy
is a BEING choice

Now it's your turn again
What have your learned so far?

29

Unconditional Love

Dogs Love

Unconditionally

The true catalyst for change

A Mastering Your Life BEING Workshop participant shared the following relationship problem with us:

> *My relationship with my wife and family couldn't be better, but my mother-in-law still gives me a hard time, treats me the same as before my transformation in the BEING Workshop. How do I get my mother-in-law to change?*

My response:

> *First, make it okay for her not to change! The only true catalyst for change is called unconditional love, which is the space you'd create for another to be who he or she is, with no intent to fix or change.*

Unconditional Love

Strange as it may seem, one of life's many paradoxes is that the true path for getting someone else to change begins with making it totally okay that they don't change. That sort of *You're okay the way you are* space created for another is called unconditional love.

Love yourself first

Of course, the change you want in another must begin with you. The rule is: you must be the change you want to see happen. If you want someone in your life to change, begin by asking yourself who YOU would be BEING if they had already changed.

The results of applying unconditional love to your relationships will amaze you. But before you can give a thing, you must first own it, so you must begin the process by loving yourself unconditionally.

The keys to the kingdom

The good life you've always wanted will be yours on that day when you have the self-confidence to claim it and the self-worth to accept it for yourself. Life really is that simple! Just get clear about what you want and then choose to BE the one who will have it.

The key to having what you want is to choose it—a simple BEING choice. Why haven't you already chosen? What stands between you and choosing the better life? My guess is that it's a self-worth issue. You haven't chosen because you have not yet made it okay for you to have it.

When, in the car dealer's showroom, you tell the salesman, *I'm just looking,* what you really mean is, *I haven't yet made it okay for me to have a new car.*

But as soon as your self-worth says it IS okay for you to have a new car, you'll know in an instant, the make, the

style, the color and the accessories you want. In the meantime, you're just stalling, waiting for your self-worth to catch up with your desires.

Self-worth decides what belongs with you, and self-confidence is what gives you the go power to choose it. Loving yourself unconditionally gives you both—self-worth and self-confidence—the keys to the kingdom. What would you choose if you had both keys to the kingdom?

What would you choose?
What would it take to make your life more complete, balanced and enjoyable?
- A happier, more loving relationship?
- Financial independence?
- Prosperous living?
- Better health?
- More time freedom for enjoying life?
- More job satisfaction?
- A true spiritual awakening?

Consider each item on this list, and ask yourself, *Would having more of this benefit improve my life?*

If you answered *Yes* to wanting improvement on one or more of these benefits, you're living a life of poverty in that way. This would be true, no matter how well off you may be in other ways.

Poverty in any of its forms is always self-inflicted. The simple way out of that form of self-imposed poverty is your determined and empowered decision to no longer put up with the condition of lack. But there's a catch… .

Unconditional Love

That benefit can and will show up in your life …but, only when and if you have the self-confidence to choose it and the self-worth to accept it.

My point here is this: what's lacking in your life is not there yet, simply because you've lacked the courage to choose it and the self-worth to accept it. The two keys to opening that door to prosperous living are self-worth and self-confidence..

I guess the question on the table for you now is: if loving yourself unconditionally would give you both keys to being prosperous—self-worth and self-confidence--are you ready to take on the job of loving yourself unconditionally?

Why love yourself first?

A line in a poem reads, *Love isn't love until you give it away.* I agree with that premise entirely, but you can't give what you don't have, can you? I'm saying you can't truly love another until you first love yourself unconditionally.

There are those who would label self-love, offensive and egotistical, but they have it backwards.

Egotism and vanity actually reveal a lack of self-love. Narcissistic behavior suggests an excessive need for admiration and approval. Contrary to popular opinion, the egotist needs acceptance, not because he loves himself, but because he doesn't.

If you thought loving yourself would make you vain, egotistical and self-absorbed, think again. Self-love simply means you accept yourself as you are, flaws and all. It means knowing that nothing about you needs to change to make you lovable. You are totally okay the way you are now. That's self-love, or in other words, unconditional love.

Unconditional love defined

Unconditional love is simply love with no conditions attached. In a relationship, it would be defined as, *the space we create for each other to be who we are.*

Think about this definition for a moment, and you'll see why you're not able to give others that quality of love (the space to be themselves, with no desire on your part to have them change).

Haven't you been thinking how much better life would be if only someone you know would change...? You can't quite see them okay the way they are, can you? That's because you don't own or haven't created that quality of space for yourself.

Love as a bargaining chip

If you don't love yourself unconditionally, it is because, as a child, you were trained with another kind of love. For most parents, unconditional love was not the norm in dealing with their children. Instead, love was used as a bargaining chip in negotiating for behavior modification.

Unfortunately, parents who unwisely offered love in exchange for good behavior, unintentionally taught kids they were not lovable. Love with conditions attached says, in effect: *When your behavior fails to match my expectations, you're not worthy of my love.*

But if you can't live up to their standards…

In growing up we set, or had standards set for us, and probably failed in our own minds to live up to those ideals. Then we came to the conclusion that, in many ways, we were just not loveable. So, under the tutelage of conditional love, the average child turns into an adult who:

- o Lacks self-confidence and self-worth.
- o Does not love him or herself.
- o Does not feel lovable.
- o Sees love as a bargaining chip to be used in negotiating the behavior modification of someone else.

If you are lacking in self-confidence or self-worth, you probably first learned about the kind of love with conditions attached from parents who had never experienced the emancipation of being loved unconditionally.

If those parents had truly understood the concept of unconditional love, they would not have used love as a bargaining chip.

Wise parents are able to express unconditional love and still teach their kids the facts of life by allowing them to learn from mistakes and that breaking the rules can have painful consequences.

God's love for you, once you truly understand it, is the perfect example of how unconditional love works so powerfully in setting you free to be you.

God's love

God gave you and me the power of choice. Along with that power, we have His promise (the unconditional love of God) that we can choose who we will be, and He will in no way meddle with our choices. In effect, He gave us *the space to be, with no intent to fix or change.*

He gave us the power of choice and set us free to make choices, good or bad, and let us learn from our mistakes.

Some would say, God's love is not unconditional because He punishes us for our sins. Sorry, God's punishment is NOT what happens when we make mistakes; instead, I say we suffer the consequence of our own ignorance—what follows our mistake is just the natural result of a not-so-wise choice.

"Sin" is a French word meaning "without"

If you're hung up on the word "sin," it might help you to know that the word "sin," originally meant "missed the mark" as in, *I aimed and missed,* or *Oops, I made a mistake.* In the adult world, we're not punished for missing the mark (for making a mistake), but we must live with the results.

In all of life, we learn by reaping benefits from wise choices, and suffering consequences when we've chosen unwisely. If you love yourself unconditionally, you will make your mistakes, smile, move on and be free to choose again. You're not bad because you shot yourself in the foot; you just made a mistake.

But if you don't love yourself unconditionally, you'll tend to beat yourself up for your mistakes, judging yourself a bad person.

I hope from reading this chapter, you've seen the light at the end of the tunnel. That light is the power to create your own reality, to be you in a whole new way!

The freedom to be you
God loves you unconditionally. Return the favor and love yourself, the Real You, that part of God in you that is experiencing life in and through you as you. Loving yourself unconditionally will set you free to be you in a brand new way.

That's unconditional love—the freedom to be you
The freedom to be you in a brand new way! Wow! If you haven't seen the light yet, you've just not allowed yourself to see just how powerful that makes you. And now that you've found it, you'll be able to shine the light of freedom to BE on others!

The path to loving yourself unconditionally
The true catalyst for any change in you or anyone else, is unconditional love. That's the space we create for another to be who he or she is without any intention to fix or change. Notice that this rule also applies to you.

If you want change in your life, you'll have to start by loving you the way you are now. Remember, you can't get to where you want to be until you've made it okay to be where you are now. Allow yourself to see that you're stuck in the status quo because you haven't made who you are now, okay.

Any change in your circumstances will require a change in consciousness. That means you will be changing your mind about who you are now and who you will choose to be. But that change in consciousness can't really happen until you create the space for it to happen.

The space to be a new you is unconditional love

At first, loving yourself unconditionally may not be easy. You've been putting yourself down, making yourself wrong all your life. "I'm not okay," has become your habitual way of thinking. Let's face it. For now, "I'm not okay" is who you are. So, attempting to love yourself as you are, unconditionally, may not fit the context of your current BEING choice.

Who would you be BEING if loving yourself unconditionally did fit?

You may find it difficult to answer that question or to choose that far outside the box in one leap. Instead of choosing to love yourself unconditionally, you might want to commit to discovering who you would be if you loved yourself as you are. You know you're not there yet, but you're choosing to find out what it would be like if you were there.

Unconditional love applied to your ego

Once you've committed to the idea of discovering what it would be like to love yourself unconditionally, you will find ways to love yourself more.

Start by making it okay that your ego resists the change you want. Talk to your ego and let it know that it is okay just the way it is now. Strange as that may seem, you've just created the space for your ego to get on the same page with you

Now, perhaps you can provide that kind of *"freedom-to-be-you"* space for another. Let's suppose you are sometimes upset by the behavior of someone near and dear to you. How does one lovingly deal with objectionable behavior in another?

Unconditional Love

The first step is to separate the person from his or her behavior. Love the person for who he or she is, and still be able to call his or her bad behavior unacceptable. Remember, the rule for manifesting a change in the quality of your life is that you, *"BE the change you want to see happen."*

When confronted with unacceptable behavior from another, first ask yourself who you would be BEING--how you would feel, if the bad behavior had already ceased? Choose to BE that person, and then create the space for that change by making it totally okay if they don't change.

This may sound like double-talk to you, but trust me, the true catalyst for change is total acceptance, without intent to fix or change. Your job is to be the person you would be if the other had already changed.

Then, once you've changed, sit back and watch the miracle happen. The other person will change to correspond to the new you because you've created the space for it to happen. You've just learned how to create a miracle!

When Joan asked me how she should deal with her fifteen-year old rebellious son in getting him to change, I gave her the above advice. She made it totally okay that he wouldn't be changing. She let him know she loved him just the way he is now and then she treated him as if he was no longer rebellious.

Joan reported back that the change in her son was nothing short of a miracle in transformation!

Remember, the miracle in your relationships starts with YOU loving YOU unconditionally.

The art of listening

Real estate salesman Sam, a top producer for his company, thought he was a good listener until he took the BEING Workshop.

During that workshop, as a participant in his Powerpact support group, he learned the art of being totally present for another, listening not only to what they were saying, but to who they were being. As a result of his new listening skills his relationships with family, friends and associates suddenly got better.

And when he *really* started listening to his clients, his sales doubled. Wow!

Selling is not telling

Before the BEING Workshop, Sam would have said that selling was about telling the prospect everything he or she needed to know to make an informed decision. And with each presentation, he'd waste very little time in getting to the point—doing the telling.

But after mastering the art of listening, Sam now says, *Selling is not telling, it's listening to what is important to the customer, listening for what his or her concerns and priorities are, and then simply answering the prospect's questions.*

The presentation is not complete until all the questions are answered. If you are truly listening, your customer will tell you exactly what it will take to make the sale. And if you have a quality product that meets his needs, he'll be helping you make the sale. Now, isn't that an easier way than what we've thought selling was?

You say you're not a salesperson?

If you think the idea of "selling is not telling" has no meaning for you because you're not a salesperson, you might want to think again.

For instance, you are selling when attempting to talk your kids into a behavior change. You are selling yourself any time you want a change of circumstances. You are selling an idea every time you communicate with others. The question is, are you really selling or just telling?

My guess, if you're like most parents, you're telling, not selling, and your kids, like most kids, won't really be listening.

In other words, they're not buying what you think you're selling. Why not? Maybe it's because you're telling instead of really listening to them. Do you listen to tell or listen to sell?

The quality of your listening is what sets the stage for "the sell" with your kids, yourself and your friends and family.

Unconditional love and listening

It might help you to think of true listening as unconditional love applied to the listening process. *Unconditional love is the space we create for another to be who they are with no intent to fix or change.*

Right now, I can hear your thoughts on that. *How the bleep do I make it okay for my kids to be who they are when I'm unhappy with their behavior?*

Here's a clue: before you discipline the child, just be sure you've separated the child from his or her unacceptable behavior!

See the child as totally okay, but the behavior as not okay. Then you can love the child and deal with his or her behavior as a separate issue. Just don't make his or her good behavior a condition of your love. In the space of total acceptance, your children will feel free to demonstrate pleasing behavior because they won't be afraid they might lose your love if they don't.

The same rules apply to all others with whom you have a relationship. Once you've learned to apply unconditional love to the listening process, the quality of all your relationships will improve beyond anything you've ever experienced. So get ready for the passion and joy that will abound in your relationships when there is certainty of your love!

When you are truly listening, you are applying unconditional love to the listening process. And while creating that quality space for another, you'll also be creating a quality space for yourself in which you just naturally grow more loving, lovable and loved.

The place to practice
In your Powerpact meetings, you'll experience that quality of space created for you by others. You'll each be transformed because you've created the space for that to happen. You see, there's far more to be gained from learning the art of listening than you might have imagined.

How do you know if you're being a good listener? Pay attention to the quality of listening you're getting from others. It is a rule of thumb that they will not be listening to you if you haven't really been listening to them. Nothing is a bigger turn-off than to talk to someone who isn't really hearing what you're saying.

If "they aren't getting you," chances are you haven't yet "heard them." Make up your mind to listen with a "new mind."

No matter who you're talking to, a child, spouse or client, the minute the other person feels that he or she is not being heard, you've lost the sale.

If you've ever had that disconnected feeling in the middle of a conversation or presentation, it's because you were not listening, and therefore telling, not selling. You are the one who broke the connection!

Prior to learning the art of listening, Sam, always an impatient listener, had the annoying habit of finishing sentences for prospects. He usually had an answer ready even before the question was asked. Now that he's learned how to listen with patience and full attention, Sam says he makes many more sales now, even though he's working far less hours than before.

Improving all your relationships

If you are a salesperson and would like to double your results while working fewer hours, make it your intention to learn the art of listening. And, as a parent, spouse, friend or associate, I can guarantee your new listening skills will improve the quality of all your relationships.

The Powerpact is the ideal space for practicing the art of listening. What you'll learn from your support group while practicing the art of supporting others and being supported will benefit all areas of your life. And it could even double your sales.

If you do not have an on-going Powerpact support group, I suggest you form one. I've heard this said many times about the Powerpact experience: *I was amazed that I could become so close, so fast, to someone I didn't know.*

Getting outside yourself

Very few people have learned the true art of listening. That's because most of us are, at some level, frightened and insecure. We're more concerned about our own needs, problems and desires than about being there for others.

To be a good listener, you must get outside yourself and be truly present for another, whether that other is family, friend or customer. Unconditional love best describes the ideal attitude for true listening. That's *the space we create for each other to be who we are, with no intent to fix or change.*

Once you truly acquire the art of true listening, every conversation you have from now on will be with the intention of having *"no intent to fix or change"*

The Art of Listening

If you are a salesperson intending to convert a prospect into a customer, or a parent or spouse hoping to convince your child or partner to behave differently, that may seem contrary to your intentions. But you'd be wise to approach the subject with an attitude of unconditional love.

The true catalyst for change

Paradoxically speaking, unconditional love is the true catalyst for change. Before the other person can or will do what you want, he or she must change who he or she is BEING. All change begins with BE and then moves on to DO and, then, HAVE.

If you have the intention of influencing the behavior of another individual, whether that person is family, friend or customer, you must first create the space for that change to take place.

The change you want, the new behavior in the other individual, the new agreement or the contract signing probably won't happen until you've created the space for it to happen—the space for his or her new way of BEING.

And again—the paradox—that sale can't really happen, until you've made it okay not to happen. If this idea sounds like reverse logic, it is! But, believe me, if you want that change of circumstances, begin by making it okay for it not to happen.

The space of unconditional love is the only true catalyst for change. It works, and it's the only thing that does!

Testing your listening skills

To test your listening skills, you might want to begin by noticing how often (or not) you are being truly listened to. If you're not listening to them, they won't be listening to you. When you talk to your significant other, your kids or prospects, how often DO you really have their full attention?

If you're talking and getting only short answers, like "yes" and "no," your significant other, child or customer is not really engaged in the conversation. You've lost the connection. And you've probably caused the 'disconnect' by not BEING there for them in the listening department.

Once that connection is broken, it may be too late to start listening!

Once you've learned the art of listening, you'll see what a difference it makes in how often you're being heard in a way that gets a positive response.

A hidden agenda?

When you are listening to him or her, notice whether or not you have a hidden agenda. Are you usually 100 percent present for others (giving him or her your full attention), or are your thoughts thinking ahead to what you will say next?

If you want to rate your listening skills, pay attention to the sort of answers you're getting to your questions. If those answers are short, mostly "yes" and "no," you may assume your listener is not really interested in what you have to say. You've already lost them. Why?

If you've not taken the time to know him or her and learn what he or she really wants, if you're not interested in what he or she has to say; why should he or she listen to you?

To get that person back to listening, try to reestablish trust with questions and patience. Ask a question such as, *Is this what you meant? Tell me more about that.* Then sit with the (often uncomfortable) empty space of silence. Really create time and space for the other to speak. Make sure he or she understands that you're intending to listen this time.

And maybe you are listening
On the other hand, if their responses are verbal and extensive, they're obviously listening and on the same page with you. Keep listening for the real questions, so you'll know which questions to answer. As your listening skills improve, watch your sales double or triple.

In acquiring listening skills, you'll want to learn what listening is and what it isn't. So let's make a list.

What listening isn't:
- o It's not about coaching.
- o It's not fixing or changing.
- o It's not problem solving.
- o It's not judging or suggesting what he or she should or shouldn't do.
- o It's not about knowing what the other person is going to say and finishing their sentences.
- o Listening is not about *"Can't wait for my turn to talk."*
- o It's not about you topping their story (one-upmanship).

What listening is:
- o Being totally present to the other party.
- o Coming to the conversation with a "fresh mind," as if you'd never met.
- o Listening is active, not passive; BE curious.
- o Asking questions for clarification.
- o Asking questions such as, *Tell me more about that or tell me so I can learn from this too.*

o Listen from a neutral place.
o Asking questions with no preconceived answer in mind
o Listening with confidence in him or her.
o Connecting with the person on the phone, or gently keeping eye contact.
o Checking back in; *Did I understand you? Is this what you meant?*

What type of questions are best?

Avoid the why question, which instead of suggesting a solution, generally gets a victim-story response. Rather, ask, "how," "who" and "what" questions.

Example: *I don't have enough time.*
Questions:
o *How much time do you need?*
o *Who would you be being if you had enough time?*
o *What would you be doing if you had enough time?*

Good question examples:
o What is possible?
o What could happen?
o What would that look like?
o Who would you be being if...?
o How could you work that to your advantage?

How does it feel when you are not listened to?

o Disenchanted?
o Resistant?
o Disconnected?
o Lacking trust?
o Not interested?

- Uncommitted?
- Sad?
- Disappointed?

If you have that disconnected feeling when in conversation with another, you probably haven't been listening. And once the connection is broken, it may be too late to start listening, or it may take a real intention to reconnect.

How do you feel when you are being truly listened to?

- Fired up!
- Uplifted!
- Energized!
- Motivated!
- Committed!
- Inspired!
- Connected!
- Relaxed!
- Comfortable!
- Confident!
- Accepted!
- Capable!

Checking your pulse

Use the above check points to help you determine if you are connected or not. When in conversation with another, check your energy. How do you feel? If either of you is not relaxed or comfortable, the connection is broken. If you feel energized, you're connected; if not, you're disconnected.

If you often have that disconnected feeling when in conversation with others, you might want to assume it's your inability to listen that is pushing people away. You have a desire to move them, but haven't taken the time to find out where they are now—what interests them, what they believe, what their questions are.

Your I already know this listening mode
One of our listening problems is that we almost always have a point of view on the subject, and we tend to listen to others through the *"I already know this" filter*. When that filter is turned on, you won't really be listening.

That would be a good time to remember, *"Selling is not telling. It's about learning what is important to the other person and answering the questions."*

And now that you know what listening is and what it isn't, what inspired action will you take?
1. Will you read this chapter again?
2. Will you choose to be a good listener?
3. Will you create a check list and notice how you're feeling about each conversation?
4. Will you notice what sort of responses you're getting?
5. All of the above?

How to respond when someone invites you to a pity party

What's a pity party?
That's one of those times in your life when you were feeling sorry for yourself as you told your tale of woe to another. We've all had our victim stories to tell. A victim story is any excuse we're using to explain why our life isn't working.

When you've told your own sad story to another (maybe over-dramatizing the situation), you were seeking sympathy. If you got it, your sympathetic friend did you no favor. A pity party never solves the problem, does it? A "poor me" story is disempowering for both the story teller and the listener.

The "victim" is asking you to agree that he is weak, powerless and incapable of solving the problem. Your agreement is not real support. Sympathy merely reinforces and adds weight to the problem.

Beyond sympathy

What's needed here is the realization that the "victim" is actually an individualization of God, temporarily denying his or her power. How do you deal with an invitation to a pity party? Don't argue or turn your to back the complainer. Listen for what's really going on beneath his or her words. Perhaps he or she is frightened, uncertain, or disappointed.

Empathy, compassion, and understanding work best as a place to start in your response to someone's victim story. Once the "victim" knows his story has been heard, you might ask when it feels right:

> *If I were to imagine you with this situation entirely solved, feeling happy and free, what would that look like, sound like, feel like for you?*

And,

> *How would it feel for you if I kept that vision in my imagination and looked forward to the day you could share with me your triumph over these circumstances?*

Wow, doesn't that feel better, being connected more deeply with the power of God within you? You bet!

Living in The Now

Now is all you'll ever have—don't waste it

Once you've stopped to consider the value of being here now, you'll realize that, for your whole life, no matter how long you live, each moment of now is all you'll ever have.

How much of your precious time do you actually spend truly enjoying your moments of now? Probably far less than you think. In fact, once you've learned from this chapter what being here now really means, I think you'll agree that you spend almost no time there!

What a waste of your most valuable asset, considering the fact that the Real You will be present only in the now!

Your past is history; you can't bring it back. And the future doesn't exist because once it gets here, it's now. Can you see that now is all you have? How dear is your "now" time for you? Do you now see why you can't afford to continue frittering it away?

Life with ego in charge

If you're wondering why you're not living your life in the now, it's because you've gone off and left your ego mind in charge of running your life. Ego was originally intended to be your faithful servant but, instead, it has assumed the role of master, hasn't it? Do you really want to leave your ego mind in command?

I don't think so. If you intend to have the quality of your life improve any time soon, I suggest you make it your intention to put the Real You in charge.

How can you tell if it's your ego or the Real You in control? Ego doesn't dwell in the now; it lives only in the past or the future. It draws its identity from the past, using the past as a filter for everything you think, hear, feel and touch. Your ego argues that it lives in the now. Believe me, it doesn't!

The past experience filter

For ego, everything happening in the now is seen through the past experience filter.

When your ego is in command, you are not being there for the present moment. Your ego mind will be focused on second-guessing some past event, or fearfully concerned about what the future may bring. Whenever your ego thoughts rule the moment, the Real You will be out of the picture.

Your True Self—the Spirit of Aliveness, Enthusiasm and Joy—will be present only in the now. Only in those moments of being truly present in the moment will you experience the reality of Being. Can you now see that a life with your ego mind in charge full time is a total waste?

If your ego has been running your life 24/7, your life has probably been an emotional roller coaster ride. But if The Real You were in charge, joy, happiness and enthusiasm would be the norm. Wouldn't you rather go for the joy?

Putting the real you in command

This chapter will show you the quickest, most empowering way to go for the joy. Your path to a higher consciousness and the better life you've always wanted begins with your enlightenment. When that awareness light comes on for you, the darkness in you disappears.

The first light of truth will dawn for you once you've realized that you are not your ego. You are, instead, a spiritual being on a path toward growing more consciously aware of your True Identity. God experiences life in and through you as you!

What is enlightenment?

Enlightenment is your inner spirit's awakening. It's the butterfly in you awakening to the reality of having wings and knowing you can fly!

Ego would have you believe enlightenment is a supernatural once-in-a-lifetime experience. But enlightenment is not a single event; it's the on-going process of growing your consciousness. Enlightenment is YOU becoming more and more consciously aware of who you really are.

You grow in consciousness only by exercising your power of choice, and by using your "Being" power to take the quality of your life to the next level.

You've been growing in consciousness all your life.
It happened:

- o When you first realized you are an individualization of God.
- o Each time you've manifested a miracle.
- o When you first realized that you were not your ego.
- o Each time you've rediscovered your power of choice.
- o Each time you have made an empowered BEING commitment that manifested the desired result (you've been doing this all your life).
- o When you realized your true identity was beyond name and form.
- o When you stepped out of separateness and into the feeling of being at-one with the Whole.

If you've been thinking enlightenment was only for the blessed special few, think again. And then choose, as your mission in life, to stay on a path toward further awakening. Realize it or not, you're already on that path, so why not ride the horse in the direction it's going, ready to see where and how far the next step up in consciousness takes you.

Believe me! Realizing this awesome truth of your being will set you free in more ways than you have yet imagined.

The meaning of the word, "Being"

The question you might want to ask yourself at this point is "How well do I comprehend the meaning of the word, "BEING"?

Have you tried to elucidate to another what you got out of the BEING Workshop? Have you had trouble explaining what you meant by the word, "Being"? Or perhaps I should ask, do you clearly understand the word "Being" enough that you could explain it to another?

It's not that easy to explain, is it? It's like trying to explain the unexplainable, isn't it? The reason "Being" is difficult to

understand is that it is not a concept ego mind can wrap itself around. "Being" is simply presence; it's an essence. It's the "I am" in you before you've added a "this" or a "that" following it.

Explaining "Being"

Describing "Being" is like trying to explain God or Spirit. You can't put Spirit in a box. It doesn't fit.

The power of God in us is called the Being Principle—as in, *"We become what we think about."* Now, that's an idea you can latch onto and understand. As our ego mind, we can easily understand that we have become what we thought about. And you might say, *"Well, that explains 'Being'."* No it doesn't!

"Being" is not a thought, an idea or a concept. Pure "Being" is "presence in the absence of thought." If you can relate to that interpretation, ask yourself who you would be being if you were being totally present in the moment and just "Being" in the absence of thought?

See if you can say "I am" without adding anything after it. See if you can experience "Being" as presence without thought.

The essence of "Being"

"Being" is an essence that cannot be boiled down into a describable image, entity or thing. You can't put God or Being in a box, because it's not a concept or a point of view; it's not even an experience. But you might say "Being" is the essence behind the experience.

For instance, have you ever:

- o Stood in wonder, admiring a beautiful sunset?
- o Watched in amazement, the miracle of birth?
- o Had that warm fuzzy feeling of gratitude in your heart?
- o Felt like you were in love with life?
- o Experienced awe as you contemplated the vastness of the Universe?
- o Felt totally at peace with the world?
- o Had a deep sense of knowing--a "can't lose" attitude?
- o Been inspired by an idea?
- o Shed tears of joy?

Of course you have. We've all had peak experiences—those times in our lives when so impressed with the majesty of the moment, all of our mind chatter stopped. During those brief, but memorable moments of wonder and joy, we were totally present in the moment, truly experiencing "BEING."

Wouldn't you like to experience more of life in the "BEING" mode?

Moments of no mind

In those fleeting timeless moments of no mind, we stepped into a different reality, paying an infrequent visit to the realm of our True Self. Can you remember how peaceful and empowered you felt at those times? And haven't you ever asked yourself if, somehow, you could take up permanent residence in that peaceful place of no mind chatter?

Think of "Being" as your very essence. It's who you are at the core—your true identity—the Real You. Think of "Being" as YOU, experiencing your own presence. It is you being that greater *"I am"* in you. It's you, acknowledging your existence; it's you saying, *"I am,"* without adding "this" or "that" after the word.

To God or As God

The intent of this "Now" Chapter is to show you how to increase in number, those peak experiences, to lengthen and broaden your awareness moments—those experiences of being truly present, alive and living in the now.

Practicing the presence

Making a habit of being present will take time and practice because that hasn't been the norm. Your ego takes its identity from the past and does not live in the present—it dwells only in the past with guilt and in fear of the future. For most of your life, your ego mind has had charge of your thoughts 24/7. Believe me, your ego wants to stay in charge.

Putting the real you in control is the purpose of this book. Are you ready to take over the reins? A simple way for you to take charge of your life is, choose to live in the now. The Real You is present only in the now, and in the now, ego is out of the picture. In that moment you are a free soul.

Can you tell me what a free soul is? It's someone who is not a slave to his/her own ideas—someone whose life is not run by ego mind. Can you even imagine spending the rest of your life without fear or worry—without ego dominance?

I doubt you can even imagine how great life could be if you were living in the now. But try. See if you can remember how you felt during one of those peak experiences, and you'll get a small taste of how awesomely wonderful life could be without ego dominance.

With this in mind (being a free soul), you might want to make it your intention, right now, to spend more and more of your life truly enjoying the wonders of a life lived in the now. Are you ready to go for the joy?

Putting spirit (the real you) back in charge

Consciousness is being aware of the truth of your BEING. As an individualization of God, you are a spiritual being experiencing life in a material reality. Your God power lies in the BEING Principle, as in, "we become what we think about." "Being," "Spirit" and "God" are synonymous.

Being present and living in the now is the conscious state but, relatively speaking, when you're living life as your ego, you are not really present. You are in an unconscious state.

Being present is a state of no mind. In that state, you are not unconscious, as in comatose or out cold, but as ego, you won't be conscious of BEING. When ego takes over, you are out of the now and have lost your true sense of being.

Living in the now

When you choose out of the role of ego mind and into that of the observer, you've put the Real You back in command. You might want to think of the times when Spirit is in charge as **you, practicing the Presence**. You accomplish this by focusing your attention on the now.

To be here now, allow yourself to be fully there for whatever's going on in the moment. You are not your thoughts or your feelings; you are the observer of those thoughts and feelings.

In the being present state, you are at peace, free of thought and yet fully alert. This state of consciousness may be difficult to maintain at first. When you're not focused on the now, thoughts will rush in, and ego mind is back in the driver's seat.

As you continue to practice living in the now, your moments of peace and tranquility will lengthen and be more easily maintained. The idea is to grow in consciousness by practicing being in the now.

You'll find it easier to create the "now" habit if you'll practice being fully conscious and present in those moments when everything in your life is running smoothly. Once you've begun to acquire the "now" habit, you'll find it much easier to step back as the observer and out of ego's fear traps.

How to begin
How do you begin the process of creating moments of now?

Experience each moment as though you had chosen it. No matter what the circumstances, instead of asking yourself why this happened to you (a victim story), appreciate what's happening as though you had intentionally chosen the experience. This approach takes you immediately outside your victim story and puts you back in charge.

Just as darkness ceases to exist in the presence of light, Being conscious while in the now creates a positive field of energy in which fear, negativity and discord cannot survive. I'm sure you can see the awesome benefit and the gain in personal power that must result from your acquiring the "now" habit.

In the now, ego mind is no longer in attendance.

Moments of no ego
In moments of no ego, you may experience:
- o Insight.
- o Enlightenment.
- o Unconditional love.
- o Being here, now.
- o Consciousness.
- o Total acceptance of what is.

Living In The Now

- o Truth.
- o Creativity.
- o Making being choices.
- o Freedom to be.
- o Surrender.
- o Being present.
- o Bliss.
- o Gratitude.
- o Commitment.

There's nothing complicated about being present. Presence is "Being" becoming conscious of itself. Consciousness is the experience of being in the moment, being self-aware.

As you practice the art of being present, your consciousness will grow and deepen. Following is a list of the advantages of living in the now—being totally conscious.

- o Living in joy.
- o A sense of BEING.
- o Being in charge of your inner space.
- o A sense of peace.
- o A sense of wholeness.
- o A feeling of aliveness.
- o Absence of ego.
- o Problems are non-existent.
- o The joy of knowing who you really are.
- o Consciousness, as opposed to unconsciousness.
- o Absence of fear.
- o Absence of worry.
- o Being totally present.
- o Feeling powerful and in charge.
- o The acceptance of what's so.

The NOW clock

In every moment of now, you have a choice: you can either choose to be totally present, in the moment, or you can let your ego mind take charge.

Remember, all you'll ever really have in life are your moments of now. Now is the only place the Real You exists. So how often will you visit the now? As a constant reminder to stay in the now, you might want to print out this NOW clock and set it up on your desk in your office.

And here's another powerful reason for your learning to live in the now: in the now there are no problems—only situations. And of course, what does the Real You do with any situation?
- o You deal with it.
- o Or you accept it as what's so and move on.

But if ego is faced with that same situation:
- ❖ It projects that situation into the future where it becomes a problem.
  - ➢ Then it sweeps the problem under the rug and hides from it.
  - ➢ Or it sets the problem up as a reason for worry.
- ❖ Or if not handled, the situation becomes your reason for feeling guilty.

Living In The Now

If you want an end to the problems in your life, don't let your ego struggle with situations when they show up. Step up to the plate and into the now; then let the Real You deal with it. In the now, you'll either handle a situation or accept it as what's so—so what!

Notice that, in becoming clear about the meaning of presence, you are being present.

Try this exercise in being present

First, choose to be totally present and alert—presence in the absence of thought. Then listen, with curious wonder, for your next thought. In being present, you are not being the thinker; you are the observer, monitoring your ego mind's activity. As the watcher, you are curiously waiting for your next thought to show up.

Of course as long as you are totally present in the moment, there will be no thought because the thinker in you is not present. So you may wait a while for that next thought to show up.

Notice, to wonder what your next thought will be, you must be present. While there in the now, allow yourself to experience the stillness of your mind and the resulting peace. Enjoy your moment of peace and make note of how long it lasts.

Notice that when your consciousness slipped below the line to unconsciousness, thoughts rushed it to fill the void and ego mind was back full tilt. With practice, you'll be able to maintain and enjoy those moments of peace for longer periods.

- Love
- Appreciate
- Confront

Sometimes love is about disturbing the peace

Every relationship has its battle zone, a no-man's-land of issues that are avoided for fear of disturbing the peace. If you have unresolved issues in a relationship, you might want to look at why you've been sidestepping any approach to the problem area. Maybe you thought:

- Confronting the issue could worsen the problem rather than resolve it.
- It could mean the end of the relationship.
- A confrontation could result in an outcome, with which you are not prepared to deal.
- The problem's resolution might be more painful than the problem.
- You might have to deal with his or her angry emotions or irrationality.
- The discussion could hurt his/her feelings.

o You might discover you are a bigger part of the problem than you want to believe.

Now let's consider the possible consequences of not addressing the avoided issues:

    o The problem could grow beyond the point of being manageable.

    o Emotions could get out of hand and blow up.

    o Failure to deal with the issue could lead to ending the relationship.

But what benefits might be gained by confronting and resolving the issue?

Allow yourself to see confrontation as a search for the truth, and then ask yourself how the relationship might be enriched if the two of you found the common ground from which you both could deal with the issue.

Wouldn't the benefits of an enriched relationship far outweigh the consequences of continued avoidance?

The first rule in solving a relationship problem: If you want the quality of the relationship to get better, you make the first move! The change you want must begin with you. BEING the change you want to see happen!

The common ground for solving relationship problems is called unconditional love. It's the space we create for each other to be who we are, with no intent to fix or change. See if you can create that kind of space for your relationship partner before you tackle the touchy relationship subject.

Creating space for another begins with the realization that everyone on this planet Earth lives in his or her own private reality. That means your view on the problem is only a small piece of the bigger puzzle. To get the whole picture, you'll want to interrogate reality from both points of view.

Your homework is to create the space for your significant other to be who he or she is with no desire or intent to fix or change. Once you've done your homework, be ready to notice, appreciate, and celebrate any positive changes in him or her.

The three keys to a healthy relationship
1. Love.
2. Appreciation.
3. Confrontation.

Of course, everyone knows a healthy relationship requires both love and appreciation, but another equally important element in keeping that relationship healthy is often missing.

That third element, necessary for maintaining a healthy loving relationship, is confrontation. If you've been avoiding the touchy issues, your relationship is not on solid ground. It's time you better understood each of the keys for keeping relationships healthy.

1: Love: True love is the space we create for each other to be who we are. That's the space of total acceptance with no intent to fix or change. You might want to ask yourself if you are offering or are experiencing total acceptance for or from your significant other.

If total acceptance is not your experience in that relationship, real love (unconditional love) may be missing from your life. And what's in its place will be something else, entirely. What most relationship partners call love is actually a sort of barter system, as in, "I'll love you if.... ."

2: Appreciation: I'm sure you appreciate your loved ones, friends and associates, but how often do you show it? Stop and think about this question for a moment. Because one of the most important things you could do to improve the quality of all your relationships would be to show each of them more of your heart-felt appreciation.

The word "appreciate," means "add value to." So, when you are expressing appreciation for your significant other, your kids, or any other relationship partners, you are truly adding real value to that person and to the relationship. Try it. Your gift of praise will be returned to you ten-fold.

When was the last time you showed someone near and dear to you that you loved and appreciated him or her? Think about it, and then decide to experiment with the process of dispensing love and appreciation on a regular basis. The high return on your investment, in terms of improving the quality of your relationships, will amaze you.

If you're seeking a way to have life get better, try this: Acquire the habit of showing sincere appreciation for others at every opportunity. Then back off and pay close attention to what shows up in the form of improved quality for all your relationships.

3: Confrontation: Most of us avoid confrontation like the plague. We side-step the delicate issues, sometimes to avoid hurting their feeling, but more often, because we're afraid we may learn we're the one at fault.

But know this: hidden issues in a relationship are thorns that just won't go away until dealt with. Like a festering splinter the avoided issue just grows worse until dug out and disposed of. If you want to improve the quality of all your relationships, find the courage to confront unresolved issues.

In approaching a touchy subject, you might want to ask,

> *What's the most important thing you and I should be talking about today?*

And then listen with a clear intent to understand his or her point of view, resolved not to defend your own.

If you really want a reality interrogation to work, questioning must be done in the space of unconditional love as described above. Then, when given an answer, ask questions that will help you get a broader view--the whole picture.

Ask questions such as,

> *Tell me more about that. I really want to know and take responsibility for how I may have caused this.*

Be prepared to hear some things you were pretending not to know. Do not, I repeat, DO NOT, at any time during the questioning, attempt to clarify your position. If you really want to know the truth, listen completely.

What are the benefits in quality listening?
- o You'll learn something of great value to the relationship.
- o You'll find the way to tackle the tough issues.
- o Removed thorns will enhance your relationship.

Dealing with an issue before it gets out of hand strengthens and enriches the relationship—creating the space for love and appreciation.

What's the danger in not interrogating reality?
A tough issue that's avoided can grow and grow until it destroys the relationship.

Are you hiding your anger?
In hiding your anger, sadness, or frustration from another for fear of upsetting him or her, you also sacrifice your capability for expressing love, joy and sincere appreciation. And, in denying your rights to own sadness, you will have also have stifled your ability to know real happiness.

Ironic isn't it? In order to be happy, you must first make it okay to be sad. But that's the truth—it's just another of life's major paradoxes.

In failing to express your true feelings, you are invalidating your God-given rights to be you. You are, in essence, denying your true identity. And since that relationship is one of the ways in which you've chosen to experience being you, how wise is it to hide the real you behind some pretense?

Never bottle up your anger; it needs an outlet. Otherwise, it gets stored in the body in some form of ache or pain. Anger also needs to be understood, because it is seldom what it seems to be. Anger is usually a cover-up for fear. Fear hides behind anger because we think it's not okay to be afraid.

In the process of confronting another person's hurtful behavior, you might just want to ask yourself what you're afraid of. What's the fear behind your anger? Allowing yourself to face your fears during the confrontation process will help you take equal responsibility for having created the problem issue.

Remember that your true purpose in confronting another is to interrogate reality—to know the truth from both perspectives. The intent for both parties is to avoid the usual ensuing right/wrong battle. To make this work, you might want to conduct your reality interrogation from the space of unconditional love.

When doing the confronting, make sure you focus on the issue and the possibility of modifying a behavior, not on changing the person or making them wrong.

When hurtful behavior goes unchallenged
The expression of anger as a quick response to someone else's upsetting behavior, is usually an ego reaction and not always the wisest course of action. But don't repress your anger. Just make sure you analyze and understand it before you express it.

You'll want to make it okay that you're angry, and then allow yourself to explore the hidden fears behind the anger. When you've taken control of your anger, express it by letting the perpetrator know that his or her unkind behavior makes you angry and is unacceptable conduct.

You'll want to confront the upsetting deed soon after it takes place, because once bad manners go unchallenged, you have just set the stage for more of the same. How so?

Each of your relationships is an unwritten agreement about who you each will be for the other. If, when the unkind act first showed up, you failed to deal with it, you established a precedent. You will have unwittingly created an agreement with him or her that this sort of hurtful behavior is now acceptable.

You can expect more of the same for as long as you continue to put up with it. How does one deal with unkind behavior?

The first step is for you to make an empowered BEING commitment to BE one who can and will confront the unacceptable behavior. Your intention is to create a new agreement that makes hurtful conduct no longer acceptable.

By challenging certain behavior as unacceptable, you will actually be doing the person a favor. How so? If that sort of unkind act hurts feelings at home, you can bet the people at work are being alienated by similar conduct.

And if abusive behavior takes place in the workplace, it will also show up at home. So, no matter how difficult it may be to hear this sort of truth about ourselves from another, there are powerful benefits to be gained in facing it.

But when confronting the perpetrator, be sure it is the behavior, not the person you are declaring unacceptable. Don't let this become a right/wrong tug of war. Make it abundantly clear, up front, that your intention is to reach a new agreement that puts an end to the hurtful conduct.

How do you proceed with the confrontation?
Your conversation might go something like this:

> *I love you, and I am angry with you.*

Or, at work, you might say,

> *I value our relationship, and I'm angry with your behavior.*

(Notice I used "and," not "but" in both examples.)

Then you could continue with something like the following:

1. *I want you to know that, _____ is hurtful behavior.*
2. *This is the effect and how I feel when you do that.*
3. *Here's what's at stake if you continue.*
4. *Here's how I've contributed to this problem.*
5. *Now tell me what your thoughts are about what I've just said.*
6. *How will this behavior change benefit your life elsewhere?*

Remember: during this confronting process, that you were party to the creation of an agreement that made the hurtful behavior acceptable.

Entering no-man's land to interrogate reality
If you think you're avoiding an issue because someone can't handle it, you're probably kidding yourself. Maybe it's time you faced up to your own fears and admit that, up until now, you've lacked the courage to deal with it.

If you've now come to the conclusion that something must change, then please realize that it is you who must change first. Before the desired change can be realized, it's you who must create the space for it to happen.

Think about how resolving this issue would enrich the relationship, and then make up your mind to deal with it! And remember: **The space for change begins with a shared willingness to interrogate reality from both points of view.**

As individualizations of God, you've each created your own reality. Your power to create a reality is the BEING Principle —*we become what we think about.*

And since you each exist in your own version of reality, you'll both see the problem from an entirely different outlook. Your reality is not the other's, so in creating space for the change you must begin with you.

You must not just be willing, but actually determined to see the problem issue from the other's point of view.

The process
Here's your step-by-step process for interrogating the other's perception of reality. But before you take the steps outlined here, you must commit to BEING the one who can and will take those steps. If you're ready for the action part, start by:

1. Naming the issue, (no blaming or finger pointing.)
2. Using an example that illustrates the situation you'd like to resolve.
3. Sharing your emotions, and how you feel about the issue.
4. Making it clear what's at stake if the issue is not resolved.

5. Letting the other know how you've contributed to the problem.
6. Indicating your desire to resolve it.
7. Inviting the other to respond.

You could begin by saying,

I've contributed to the problem by not letting you know, before now, how much this upsets me. Instead, I've withdrawn, and as a result, our relationship has suffered. For that, I am truly sorry.

Then indicate your wish to resolve the issue by saying,

Please make me understand the problem from your perspective. I really want to know, so we can reach a common ground from which to resolve the issue.

Notice that in using this approach, there has been no attack. Instead, you will have described your version of reality on the issue, making it clear that your reality is just one half of the whole truth.

8. Asking questions to learn more about the other's point of view.

In this step, most of the conversation will take place. This is where you'll hear things about which you may strongly disagree. If you really intend to resolve the issue, please don't step in and attempt to defend your own reality concept.

Don't let your ego take over here

Remember, this is a reality check. This is your time to shut up and simply listen and learn. This is your chance to really understand the other's view on the issue. Ask questions at this point. Do perception checks, such as:

Can I tell you what I'm hearing? Is that what you're saying?

The point here is not to be satisfied with what's on the surface. Ask the other,

Tell me more about this. I see it quite differently, and I really want to understand. Tell me how you came to this conclusion.

9. Reviewing what you've learned.

What have you learned, and where does that leave you? Is there more to be said? What's needed to resolve the issue, now that you've reached this new level of understanding? How do you resolve it and create a happy ending to this conversation?

10. Make a new agreement about who each of you will be for the other and decide together how you will hold each other accountable in keeping the agreement.

For more information on interrogating reality, you might want to read *Fierce Conversations* by Susan Scott

It really takes all three:

- **Love**
- **Appreciate**
- **Confront**

But can you handle the confront?

Once You "Get IT"

I got it!

Once you get it

Many years ago, I participated in a week-end workshop called, "The Training of New Mexico." On the Sunday evening at the conclusion of a long week-end, training graduates greeted each other with a loving hug, a knowing smile, and the words, *I got it.*

Unfortunately, in that moment of *I got it,* they just lost it, because what they were experiencing in that moment of enthusiasm—in the moment of revelation—was the presence of God expressing in and through them as them—as a knowing they had never experienced before.

It was just one step up

They had just taken one step up on the grand stairway of self-discovery, and they were looking at life from a whole new, awesome perspective. But then they, quite naturally and desperately, wanted to share their newly found joy and enthusiasm with everyone who would listen.

So then they tried to describe their experience—to conceptualize it so they could tell others what they had "gotten," and in the moment of making IT a concept, lost it.

When I read Think and Grow Rich, by Napoleon Hill, I "got it" big time and what I "got" transformed the quality of my life forever after. I couldn't wait to share my newly discovered truth about life: *we become what we think about.*

I bought every copy of that book in town —17 copies—and proceeded to give "Think And Grow Rich" to all my friends, telling them, *this book is what you need. It will change your life.*

Big disappointment
At the time of my gift giving, I doubt any of them "got it," and some of them actually resented the gift, asking me,

> *What makes you think I need to change? Is there something wrong with me?*

I'm suggesting you may have the same experience.

If you really want to recommend this book, tell them how it transformed your life, and leave it at that.

Don't try to sell them on why they need to read this book. Once they've seen the change in you—your new enthusiasm for life—they'll want to have what you have and decide on their own, they must have the book.

The problem with *I got it* is that you and I are programmed to have amnesia. So, just as soon as you "get it" you'll lose it, unless you've hired yourself a coach who will remind you, from time to time, that life is a journey, not a destination—a coach who will help you remember that you DO have the power to choose again.

If you've decided not to be stuck in any new box for long, you will make this agreement with your coach; you'll do this, because you've committed to your continued growth in consciousness.

You'll know that each step up on that grand stairway to a higher consciousness gives you an even grander view of life. You'll know that you'll finally *get it* big time once you have nothing left to prove.

You'll arrive at that place in consciousness where you've concluded that enough is enough. At that point the Game will no longer be about you, it will be about them and about making a difference.

Life is a game, the purpose of which is self-discovery. When you can stop taking yourself and life so seriously, you will deal with life as a game.

That's when you'll treat each win—each step up in consciousness—as just one more trip around the game board in the grand Game of Life. You and your coach will then be planning your next out-of-the-box adventure.

Once you've acquired the winner's attitude—the winning Spirit—you'll just keep winning and winning. At that point, you will have become a shining model for success, proving by example that life is nothing more complicated than a BEING choice.

Why does having the winner's attitude make you a certain winner?

To really understand it, you must realize that belief in one's self and belief in God are synonymous. Once you've arrived at that sense of certainty—that knowing feeling—your can't-lose attitude, you will have become, in that moment, one with God, and as such cannot fail, no matter what you attempt.

If that sounds sacrilegious to you, sorry but you are, in fact, an individualization of God, and that makes you invincible once you've put the Real You in charge.

How does one acquire a winner's attitude?

- It begins with making it okay to fail.
- Then in having the courage (Spirit) to do what you feared doing.
- You'll grow more confident with each successful venture outside the box, so--
- Be willing to learn from your mistakes.
- Keep on doing it, until you get it right.
- With each success you'll acquire more of the winner's attitude—that sense of certainty that allows you to know you can't fail.
- Play at life as though it were a game because, believe me, that's what it is!

And one final word, a quote from Emerson, who once said,

Get your bloated nothingness out of the way
and let the divine circuit come through!

Testimony

What they're saying is, "It really works!"
Although the following testimonies are praise for another book and for the BEING Workshop, you may want to read it as real testimony for how powerful and life-changing the ideas in this book could be for you.

All of the following testifiers are graduates or present participants of the six-month Mastering Your Life BEING Workshop. The ideas for this book were created, tested and proven to work during their participation in that workshop.

Their testimony is living proof that the life-changing lessons to be learned from reading this book can alter the quality of your life for the better forever. It's not just theory. It really works.

If you are truly ready for a change, what you'll learn from reading this book will give you results similar to those in the following success stories.

❧⊱⊰❧

The greatest thing I learned from Darel and <u>Being The Solution</u> is how the Creative Process really works.

Most people live their life process like... Do, Have and then Be. But if you want your life to really work and have a quantum leap in results, you must live your life process beginning with, Be, Do and then Have. You see, you must BE that person first, then you will DO the inspired action naturally and then you will just naturally HAVE what you want. But you have to make a BEING CHOICE first then the DOING will follow.

Don't just go out there and DO, DO, DO. Using the BE DO HAVE success formula, I was able to believe and achieve—manifest any end result I wanted. I went from earning $750,000 per year to over $1,000,000 per month. Thanks Darel.

—Thach Nguyen

❧◦❧

My quality of life has improved significantly in many areas of my life since completing the Being Workshop. The greatest improvement of all has been the feeling of just knowing the people and things I want in my life will automatically come to me...and they are.

I now have a deep sense of inner peace and my relationships have improved beyond words. I am DOING less work and making more money than ever before. I've recommended the BEING Workshop and your books to my closest friends and I would suggest them to anyone seeking spiritual and financial freedom. I'm looking forward to the next few years of education with you!

—Chris Larmer

❧◦❧

For over 8 years, I've been learning from and practicing use of the abundance tools the BEING THE SOLUTION workshops offer. And life just keeps getting better and better.

I have become someone I once only dreamed about. And I intend to keep studying, perfecting and growing with this information. My life continues to unfold abundantly and always by my own design as I assist others through the process of BEcoming their dreams as well.

--Deborah Ivanoff

ಎಲ್ಲಿ

Thank you so much for all that you have done for me and my ego. The BEING CHOICE!!!!

--Eric Elegado

ಎಲ್ಲಿ

Now I know what life is about!

Prior to reading <u>Being The Solution</u>, I was a goal writing machine working day and night to get ahead. Now that I practice Darel's techniques, I am experiencing a quantum leap in production while working significantly fewer hours. I never imagined that I could 'Advance to Go' and collect my $200 so easy. I can't wait for his next lesson.

--Greg Harrelson

ಎಲ್ಲಿ

Since I first took the BEING Workshop less than three years ago, my net income has tripled, and my net worth has more than doubled. All of this has happened with far less stress in my life. That's why I continue to practice the BEING principles and have taken the workshop numerous times! Regards, Jackie

--Jackie Pasciak

಄ஃ

Since working with Darel (and Deborah), I have experienced such growth in my business and investments that I have decided to retire in 3 year. (I am 37 now). Even better than that is the growth I've experienced in my life as a person, allowing that light that burns in all of us, to shine!

--James Tjoa

಄ஃ

Shannan and I would like to express our thanks for allowing us to be a part of this "Being the Solution" workshop. The results that have shown up have been absolutely phenomenal!!! I would like to share a few, that have had the biggest overall impact in our lives.

First and foremost, the biggest break through that the two of us have had is with our relationship with our own being with ourselves. In the past our lives would be going along and there would be stress and worry even when there was nothing to get worked up about.

This seems odd to me now; however this was a constant and I've come to learn that everyone of us from all walks of life have to deal with this daily. The break through has come in the many techniques that you've shared with us. Learning that EGO doesn't have to run the show and just "being" is the real joy in life has removed the day to day stress and worry. Not to be totally cliché, but this is a priceless feeling.

Everyone has heard about living life feeling joy within and not to worry or be stressed, because that never solves anything anyway! However up until working with you, living that way escaped us. Learning that those two feelings (worry and stress) are just Ego's play on running the game and not truly how we choose to live has been our greatest gift.

This has opened up a life that is purely joyful. We now are free to choose rather then do things we do not want to do but were doing out of guilt or from some other lesser feeling. How has this affected our overall life?

Well, our relationship with each other is and now has been off the charts great for this past year. We can share things with each other that before may have provoked a lot of tension and even some petty fights. We now have the freedom to renegotiate what our needs are and what works / doesn't work for us individually in the relationship.

This freedom, comfort and closeness have subsequently branched out into our other relationships with my children. I now can communicate with them on another level and help them see Ego's game. I am able to give them the tools to dance with Ego's worries rather then struggle with the mind's stress or even worse wait until they are all grown up to learn it, if they're lucky.

My closeness with, my children, Tyler and Emily is absolutely enviable and I have the pleasure of other parents asking what I do with them to create the relationship this way. When I answer it's in our being and coming from that state; naturally they look puzzled.

Shannan's closeness with Tyler and Emily has always been good and I have witnessed it go to another level of intimacy. This all comes from the freedom to be at peace and leave the worries behind. One never knows what price is paid by carrying the stress and worries around until you leave them behind and experience what is available in life when the being choice is peace and free.

As far as how this has impacted us in our business? Well we have experienced how much clearer thinking and communication is with a peaceful being. When that is in place it seems the whole world of opportunity has opened up and we are free to see it vs. operating with the blinders on.

To put it straight, we have earned more in 45 days than we did all of last year. What's truly great is that the income we earned last year is in the top 1% nationally. So, we are grateful that we can now earn this and more in a fraction of the time and without the grind it out feeling!

To God or As God

To put it directly; we have always kind of known we've had a great life. We now have the tools to fully and freely enjoy it and be at peace!!!

Thank you from the true being within our hearts!
                                        --Joe DiRaffaele
                                        --Shannan Fogle

∽∾∽

I began the Being Workshop shortly after a difficult and traumatic divorce. I had a struggling, cash strapped business which I needed to turn around. I knew that my old patterns of thinking and feeling would prevent my moving forward. I decided to enroll in the Being Solution and change my inner landscape

Since embracing the Being Solution I have discovered my power to create my life, transform my self image and propel my business forward. My sales are up almost 50%, I've found a great manager, and I am moving to a new location three times bigger than my current one. I have also discovered a new career to pursue. But most importantly I have acquired a new sense of myself, embraced abundance consciousness, and feel in tune with life.
                                        --Judy Banfield

∽∾∽

Taking the BEING THE SOLUTION Workshop had me take responsibility for what I say and what's in my life. A newer relationship evolved into a wonderful, loving, committed marriage because of the growth I experience

Testimony

while in BEING THE SOLUTION. I manifest the money or house I ask for, because I let go of ego resistance.

--Scott Friedman

৵৽

Darel has shown me the previously-hidden "inward path." Since employing his philosophy and principles, life has made a marvelous tilt; I am now experiencing true fulfillment in every phase and magnetically attracting things I thought mostly belonged to others - money, opportunity, rewarding relationships and stratospheric personal strength.

--Scott B. Umstead

৵৽

Since I've started in the workshop, the huge difference is that I do not worry about things anymore. Worry used to consume me. Not anymore. I live my life in a free mode. I know I can do what I want to.

--Tamara Dean

৵৽....

To say that you changed my life is an understatement. Life changing friends that I will have for a lifetime is just one of the benefits of doing the BEING Workshop! Deciding to give 110% was the best thing that has ever happened to me in all my 31 years.

I not only enjoy more money, working a whole lot less, I enjoy my family, my career and my co-workers 500% more. I now completely enjoy all aspects of my life. I've pretty much reduced my stress to NONE and am now at peace with life. I have not felt this carefree since I was a child.

Phenomenal things are happening all around me, only now I have the time to see and enjoy them! You, Darel, Deborah, and Sherry you have changed my life in every positive way that it could have been changed! I am forever grateful to you for showing me all the joy and light that was within me all along!!

You will be one of the major stepping stones to life changing events that I'll tell all my grandkids about! It is a gift to know that there are people in the world today willing to give it their all to show us just how wonderful life really can be. You all are truly the biggest blessing that has ever happened to me. I love you guys!! :)

-- Tammie Johnson

ಶಾಶ

Darel,
I am honored to have been a part of the workshop that created this book. You have given me tools to live the life I've always dreamed of having. Now I have peace, profit, love, abundance, acceptance, and I'm making a difference. I'm not holding back on anything in life.

You truly made a difference in my life. I thank GOD daily for putting you into my life. I wish everyone could learn these life changing principles.

--Venny Saucedo

To learn more about the BEING Workshop, you'll find contact information on the next page

Contact Information

To share what you "got" with friends—before you buy more of this book—you might want to check out volume discounts available. www.ToGodOrAsGod.com

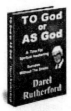

To purchase audio book go to
www.ToGodOrAsGod.com

Other books you might want to read:

So, Why Aren't You Rich?
Darel Rutherford

BEING THE SOLUTION
Darel Rutherford

For workshop information and schedule
email darel@richbits.com
or visit www.ToGodOrAsGod.com
To schedule coaching, call 505 280 0930